Sign Language Made Simple

Second Edition

Edgar D. Lawrence

Introduction by Ruth A. Reppert

Illustrator / Mike Johnson

Springfield, Missouri
02-0500

Dedicated to the Memory of
Alan Terpening
1952–1974

He is affectionately remembered as director of the Living
Signs Choir (Central Bible College), an interpreter, a
friend, and a Christian whose total dedication to people
who are deaf left a lasting impression on all who knew
him.

Illustration by John H. Green

A closed captioned video of *Sign Language Made Simple,* featuring two hours of signing instructions
covering all thirty lessons, is available from Gospel Publishing House (order no. 26-0110).

First edition published 1975.
Second edition 1999.

Library of Congress Cataloging-in-Publication Data

Lawrence, Edgar D.
  Sign language made simple / Edgar D. Lawrence ; graphic design, Mike Johnson.—2nd ed.
      p. cm.
  Includes bibliographical references and index
  ISBN 0-88243-500-0
  1. American Sign Language.   I. Title.
HV2474.L38   1998
419—dc21   96-6501
                                                                                       CIP

Printed in the United States of America

Table of Contents

Acknowledgments

Special thanks to Robert and Ruth Reppert. Ruth has used this book as a sign language instruction text ever since it was published. Also, she has enhanced the book by beautifully and succinctly revising and updating the introductory material for this second edition. Robert and Ruth have unselfishly produced the video of *Sign Language Made Simple,* totally at their expense. The video has increased the usability of this book. Ruth's lifelong experience with Deaf people has given a very positive addition to the entire book, and her gracious willingness to share ideas, methods, and experience with all who use this book is gratefully and humbly acknowledged.

A special thanks to the present staff of Book Editing at Gospel Publishing House who have worked on this book, particularly Stacie Agee, Jean Lawson, and Leta Sapp. Their many hours of meticulous work updating, refining, improving, and reorganizing the book can never be adequately rewarded. A thank you to each of you. And thanks to Missie Huffman, Mike Mills, and Thomas Sanders at Gospel Publishing House who helped coordinate the work, and to Lance Smith who drew new signs for the second edition.

Particular mention and appreciation are due to many people who helped make the first edition a reality: Jacob Trout, Eldon Post, Jeanne Manning, Edward and Charlotte Graham, Mike Johnson, Richard Slaton, the Board of Administration and students of Central Bible College, Jack Green, David J. Johnston, Wayne Warner, and Janice and Fred Gravatt.

Special recognition needs to be given to Marty Feldy for his assistance through the years.

Great appreciation is expressed to the students who have used this book and offered suggestions that have resulted in a book of increased usability.

A book of this nature obviously represents endless hours of work—hours that were taken from my normal family activities. Therefore, I offer a special word of appreciation to my wife, Delna, and my children, Jim, Starla, Paul, and Rhonda.

Deafness and Sign Language

William F. Ross III

The following excerpt from *Deaf in America* challenges many existing ideas and assumptions about deafness and people who are deaf.

> The traditional way of writing about Deaf people is to focus on the fact of their condition—that they do not hear—and to interpret all other aspects of their lives as consequences of this fact. Our goal in this book is to write about Deaf people in a new and different way. In contrast to the long history of writings that treat them as medical cases, or as people with "disabilities," who "compensate" for their deafness by using sign language, we want to portray the lives they live, their art and performances, their everyday talk, their shared myths, and the lessons they teach one another. We have always felt that the attention given to the physical condition of not hearing has obscured far more interesting facets of Deaf people's lives (C. Padden, and T. Humphries, *Deaf in America: Voices from a Culture* [Cambridge: Harvard University Press, 1988], 1).

For years the public has focused on the inabibity of deaf people to hear, but the focus is now shifting to the language of the American Deaf—the language of signs. You cannot separate sign language from the native users of that language, culturally Deaf.*

Since attitudes toward deafness, the Deaf, and sign language have changed so much, deaf education also is having to make some changes. These involve the methods used to teach children who are deaf. The question that is being proposed is, Which method of signed communication (language) would be best for educating children who are deaf?

The educational issues that at one time may have appeared to be so black and white are now many shades of gray. No one educational method is the solution for all children and adults. The concept of total communication was born from the understanding that not all people were created equal. In a nutshell, total communication is using whatever methods are effective for learning to occur. The issue should not be whether to use American Sign Language (ASL) or another form of signed English, or whether to include teaching on Deaf culture. The issue should be, Is the school that these children attend able to offer a complete program? It is very important that teachers of children who are deaf keep in mind that these children will one day grow up and become adults who are deaf.

---

*The word *Deaf* capitalized refers to those deaf individuals who identify with Deaf culture and Deaf community and use sign language to communicate. Some people who are deaf identify with the hearing community and generally do not use sign language.

For a greater understanding of Deaf culture and the Deaf, see the following readings.

Gannon, J. *Deaf Heritage: A Narrative History of Deaf America.* Silver Springs, MD: National Association of the Deaf, 1981.

Lane, H. *When the Mind Hears: A History of the Deaf.* New York: Random House, 1989.

Lieberth, A. "Rehabilitative Issues in the Bilingual Education of Deaf Children." *J.A.R.A.* 23 (1990): 53–61.

Mindel, E., and M. Vernon, eds. *They Grow in Silence: Understanding Deaf Children and Adults.* 2d ed. Boston: College-Hill Press, 1987.

Moores, D. F. *Educating the Deaf: Psychology, Principles, and Practices.* 3d ed. Boston: Houghton Mifflin Company, 1987.

Padden, C., and T. Humphries. *Deaf in America: Voices from a Culture.* Cambridge, MA: Harvard University Press, 1988.

Rutherford, S. "The Culture of the American Deaf." *Sign Language Studies* 59 (1988): 129–147.

Schunhoff, H. "Slow. Road Slippery When Wet." *DCARA News* 15, no. 10 (1995): 3,8.

Van Cleve, J. V., and B. A. Crouch. *A Place of Their Own: Creating the Deaf Community in America.* Washington: Gallaudet University Press, 1989.

Vernon, M., and J. F. Andrews. *The Psychology of Deafness: Understanding Deaf and Hard-of-Hearing People.* New York: Longman, 1990.

Preface to the Second Edition

How does this book differ from most other sign language books available today? Unlike a reference book or dictionary, *Sign Language Made Simple* is like a textbook. A beginning reading textbook, for example, begins with simple words and pictures and proceeds to add new words to the ones already mastered in previous lessons. *Sign Language Made Simple* is arranged similarly.

The signs in this book are presented in the context of English sentences, with a graphic drawing of each sign placed above the English word it represents. Although American Sign Language (ASL) has a sign order that differs from English, most Deaf people use their signs in English word order when conversing with a hearing person. This method of sign communication is called Pidgin Sign English (PSE).

Designed with the beginner in mind, *Sign Language Made Simple* will teach sign language from a contextual sentence format. The main purpose of the sentences is to give the student a large vocabulary that already has a contextual basis. Once the vocabulary is established, interaction with those who are deaf will build a foundation base from which ASL and conceptual signing will flow. That is why the book is called *Sign Language Made Simple*.

The six hundred sentences in signs that make up the thirty lessons in this book have been used in a classroom setting since 1968, with the instructor demonstrating the signs. The inspiration to place these sentences in graphic art came from watching preschool children sign stories that had been pictured in signed English. It seemed reasonable that if children could learn the language of signs by looking at pictures, surely adults could do the same. This book can be used in a classroom setting or for individual study.

A special feature of the book is the final section presenting signs for vocabulary used in some church settings. It makes the book useful in both secular settings (high schools, colleges, universities, continuing education programs, etc.) and in church and church-related settings (Bible colleges, camps, seminars, etc.).

The second edition has some new features to help with learning sign language. In addition to updating some of the signs and adding some signs, the new signs in each lesson are noted with a check mark. The words for these signs are also listed at the end of the lesson in a table. Each lesson now has twenty-four additional sentences that can be used to practice the signs from the lesson.

Introduction

Ruth A. Reppert

Welcome to the community of people who have chosen to pursue a practical and rewarding goal—the learning of sign language—that has taken them beyond their expectations: individuals have come to enjoy deeper relationships with Deaf neighbors and family members; classmates have reached new heights of communication with Deaf peers; employees have made lifelong friends of Deaf coworkers; and many sign language students have gone forward to become professional workers with the Deaf. Welcome to the potential of going beyond your own expectations.

Perhaps you wonder exactly how many deaf people use sign. "The latest published data for the U.S. come from the National Health Survey of 1991. It shows rates per 1,000 population as 8.6 for hearing impairment, 5.7 for deafness of all ages at onset, 1.3 for deafness before 19 years of age, and 0.8 for prelingual deafness (each rate for deafness includes all earlier ages)."[1] Please note that these are estimates; "no one has actually done a study of persons who use sign to communicate"[2] and since the number "differs" by geographical location and over time, we "do not apply a national rate to a specific part of that nation," expecting to arrive at an exact number. To arrive at a guesstimate of the number of Deaf people who live in your area and with whom you may communicate using the signing skills gleaned from this book, you will need to do some investigating of your own. You may inquire of your local school or college, the phone company's department for persons with disabilities, the state relay service, a local Deaf service center, a local interpreter's group, etc.

Whether your goal is to acquire conversational skills or your aim is to advance beyond that, you will find that this book offers a tried and true method of learning to sign in a format that makes learning rapid and simple: the signs of American Sign Language are placed in English word order, a

---

[1] The population that has hearing impairment includes two groups: those who are *deaf* and those who are *hard-of-hearing*. If a person has the ability to hear and understand spoken language only if aided by amplification and/or speech reading, that person is hard-of-hearing. If a person is unable to hear and understand spoken language, even with amplification, that person is deaf.

[2] Quotations in this paragraph are taken from an e-mail correspondence with Dr. Jerome D. Schein, noted researcher and writer on deafness issues, and are included here with his permission.

contact signing mode used by Deaf people in America when communicating with those who are non-deaf. This approach allows you to sign communicate from the very first lesson.

The signs introduced in the first few lessons deal with common, everyday expressions, such as, "Hello." "How are you?" "I am fine." As the lessons proceed, new signs are presented in sentences that include previously introduced sign vocabulary. It is this ongoing natural review that makes the learning task simple. You may find, however, that your early efforts seem awkward, and you might have initial difficulty in managing your hands, arms, and fingers. Do keep in mind that your fluency in signing and fingerspelling will improve as you practice. The more often you practice, the faster you progress. The first time you succeed in a signed conversation with someone who is Deaf, you will surely feel that it has been well worth your efforts.

Using the practice videotape that complements this book is highly recommended. It demonstrates each of the six hundred sentences and provides an at-home tutor and practice partner. You can rewind and repeat sections as you desire and are free to time the practice session to fit into your schedule. The video is useful for independent study and will increase your fluency, accuracy, and retention of the signs. (See page 2 for information on ordering the videotape.)

Not surprisingly, just as there are regional variations in English words, there are regional variations in signs. The most widely used signs are presented here. As you mingle and communicate with a variety of Deaf people, you will learn other variations of signs for the same English words. When you encounter a different sign, do not ponder which sign is correct; add it to your storehouse of sign vocabulary. Knowledge of sign variations adds to your flexibility and capability in expressing and understanding signed communication.

As you progress through this book, you will discover that American Sign Language is not limited to signs and fingerspelling, but includes nonmanual ingredients such as facial expression and gesture. Use of these nonmanual movements as you sign is encouraged. They enhance meaning and promote clear understanding. You will also discover that one English word may be represented by several different signs, depending on the meaning of the word in context. Conversely, one sign may be expressed by various English words, again, based on the meaning or concept of the sign. Be open to new ideas and concepts and you will enjoy this new adventure.

Total communication is communication that may include the use of all forms of communication: gestures, signs, speech, speechreading, fingerspelling, and when necessary, reading and writing. Through the use of the entire spectrum of language modes, the full message and accurate understanding are more likely to occur as compared to the use of a limited mode. The objective is to reduce the amount of guesswork necessary to decipher the message and, thus, to eliminate misunderstanding.

You may learn to sign, but remember that your signing is only 50 percent of the communication; you must also learn to understand those who sign to you. Acquiring skills in signed communication and understanding those who use it requires associating with persons who are Deaf whenever you can. Seek out places in your community where Deaf people congregate—contact a deaf service center or a speech and hearing organization. You may find such places in the telephone directory.

Now get ready for easy learning and enjoyment as you proceed to acquire signing skills for conversing with those who are Deaf. This book will provide all the helps you will need along the way.

Using This Book

Ruth A. Reppert and Edgar D. Lawrence

Accurate execution of the sign is crucial. The handshape, placement in relation to the body, orientation of the palm, movement, direction, and intensity all help convey the concept. Even the slightest deviation may result in your signing a completely different concept or no concept at all. The graphics, lines, and arrows in the sign illustrations in this book clarify placement, orientation, and movement.

Signs

Basically, signs are made comfortably. Exaggerated signs are ugly. Some signs come from the wrist, some from the elbow, and some from the shoulder. Signs dealing with concepts that center on the mind or head are all signed from the head. Emotions come from the heart and, therefore, are signed from the heart.

did

If a sign is signed with one hand, use your dominant hand. If it is signed with two hands, then you may be doing identical action with both hands (for example, the first sign for *did*), or two different actions. If each hand is doing a different action, use your dominant hand for the larger movement (for *work*). Refer to the Instruction Symbols key for clarification on the movements.

Speech is often used when signing so that people who are deaf or hard-of-hearing may read your lips and use any residual hearing they may have.

R-on-L / 2X
work

New Signs

New signs in each lesson have a check mark below the sign illustration. The words for the new signs are also listed at the end of the lessons in the New Signs List. You will want to pay special attention to these signs and use them in the practice sentences to increase your retention of them.

√

BHA
book

The index at the back of the book lists the lesson and sentence number for the first time the sign is used in the book.

English Signs

English sign systems have invented signs to represent English words. The primary purpose of these signs is to teach English to children who are deaf. In conversation, signs representing English words such as *a, an the, of, be, it, are, was, were,* and the infinitive *to* often are not used when they are unnecessary for communicating the thought. However, they may sometimes be fingerspelled to clarify meaning. For this reason, you will sometimes find a word that does not have a sign graphic above it, while at other times the word may be fingerspelled.

English sign systems have altered signs of American Sign Language by adding movements to represent prefixes, suffixes, tense markers, and other elements of English. Every effort has been made here to avoid using these altered signs because they are generally not used by Deaf people in conversation.

Sign Illustrations

Illustrations with two signs show either (1) the two most common signs in use or (2) two common signs for that word that have different conceptual meanings. An example of a word with two signs is the entry for *talk.*

2X / BHA / AA
talk

Drawings of signs do not always depict the same view or angle. This is to show the clearest view possible for your immediate understanding. The face and body are not always illustrated, but if you execute the sign as shown, your hands should be in proper placement.

Facial Expression

Facial expression replaces vocal intonation in expressing the feeling or flavor of the message. The face may show surprise, sadness, seriousness, urgency—virtually any emotion that may underlie the message. Signing with a blank facial expression is like speaking in a monotone. As you acquire more and more sign vocabulary, you will be better able to add facial expression to enhance the meaning.

F-X
?

Questions are conveyed through facial expression by raising eyebrows in a quizzical fashion. Sometimes this expression is accompanied by leaning forward in expectation of an answer and by gesturing with both palms up. "F-X" above the question mark in a sentence is there to remind you to use Facial eXpression and appropriate posturing.

Indexing

Pointing the index finger, "indexing," is done for pronouns (*he, she, it, me, you, they, them, her, him*, etc.), for adverbs (*there, here, up, down*, etc.), and for the preposition *at* (*at home, at school, at the doctor's office*). When you are indexing, the finger points to the subject, person, place, or thing.

Possessives

Possessives—*my, your, his, hers, ours, theirs*, etc.—are always indicated by the flat hand, the palm thrusting toward the person who is in possession. For *my* or *mine*, you actually rest the palm on your chest.

R-on-B
mine
my
[touch chest]

Sign Movement

Sign movement often adds meaning to a sign.

❏ Direction: Moving the sign for *give* away from yourself to someone else shows that you give to someone; moving the sign toward yourself shows that someone gives to you.

❏ Speed and Strength: The speed at which a sign is made can show a gentle (slow) breeze or a fierce (fast) windstorm. The sign for *walk* done with strong strokes may show the march of a soldier, while a *walk* with gentle strokes may indicate a leisurely stroll.

❏ Repetition: Repeating a sign several times conveys a length of time. For example, *sit, sit, sit* indicates sitting for a long of time.

have
(possessive)

Clarifying Words

Notations in parentheses below an entry clarify which meaning of the word is being used. Conceptual accuracy of the sign conveys the meaning of the message. For example, a different sign for *have* would be used in the following sentences: "I have a frog" (possessive). "They have saved enough money for a vacation" (completed action).

have
(completed action)

Instruction Symbols

Instruction symbols give further information for executing the signs, like the direction the sign moves, the hand to be used, where the hands are placed. Following is a list of the symbols used. You may wish to adapt this key if you are left-handed. In that case, you would reverse the references, substituting L for R and R for L.

WA
seem like
appear, look like

✔	New sign
1X	Action one time
2X	Repeat the action twice
AA	Alternating action
BHA	Both hands do the action
C-C-W	Counterclockwise (to the person signing)
CW	Clockwise (to the person signing)
EA	Elbow action (action from the elbow)
F→B	Front toward the body
F→L	Front of body to left
F→R	Front of body to right
F-X	Facial expression (for questions)
IN	In toward the body
→L	To left
L→B	From left toward the body
LHA	Left hand action only
L-in-R	Left hand in right
L-on-R	Left hand on right
L→R	Left to right
OUT	Away from the body
R	Right hand
→R	To right
R→B	From right toward the body
R→F	Right hand moves forward
RHA	Right hand action only
R-in-L	Right hand in left
RL	Right hand across left
R→L	Right hand to left
R-O-L	Right hand over left
R-on-B	Right hand on body
R-on-L	Right hand on left
R-U-L	Right hand under left
WA	Wrist action
WF	Wiggle fingers

Memory Aids

Memory aids are based on the principle of association, which enhances retention in memory. Memory aids are found below a main word in black Roman type and also at the end of each lesson in the New Signs List. For example, under the word *cat* you will find "whiskers," which the sign seems to represent. Or a phrase may be given to make it easier for you to recall the configuration of that sign; for example, for the word *understand*, the phrase "light goes on" is given.

Synonyms

Synonyms are printed in purple under a main purple-lettered word, indicating that the sign depicted for the main word is used for all of these words. For example, the entry containing *look* has the words "appear" and "seem" in purple under it. The same sign will be used for all three words. Synonyms are included in the index.

Instruction Words

Instruction words are in brackets below an entry and explain how to execute the sign; for example, "[fingers stroke nose]" under the entry *funny* means to stroke your nose when you are signing the word.

WA / 2X
cat
whiskers

RHA
understand
recognize
light goes on

WA
look
appear, seem

2X
funny
[finger stroke nose]

Fingerspelling

The Fingerspelling Practice Drills at the end of each lesson will give you practice words with similar letter combinations. This enables you to become so familiar with the hand configurations that your eye will recognize them instantly when someone fingerspells to you. Repetition and practice will increase your speed and fluency.

Words that are fingerspelled when signing usually have no sign; however, some words, such as *do, did, at, on, in, be,* and *it,* can be spelled almost as easily as signed since they are short.

When you fingerspell words with double letters, like *b-o-o-k,* sign the first "o" and then move your hand slightly to the right and then spell the rest of the word.

O

Also, practice the signed numbers, which are fully illustrated at the end of this section, until you can instantly recognize them.

Fingerspelling Hints

❑ Relax your arm and fingers.
❑ Hold your hand in a comfortable position in front of your body at about shoulder level near the chin where both the lips and the hand may be clearly seen.
❑ Face your palm outward.
❑ Do not bounce the hand or arm.
❑ When fingerspelling two or more words consecutively, hold the last letter of one word for a brief moment (pause) before spelling the next word.
❑ Do not practice forming the alphabet in A-B-C order, but practice by fingerspelling words.
❑ Pronounce the words phonetically (make the sounds of the syllables) with your voice when you are fingerspelling, and mentally when you are reading fingerspelled words. Although you may misspell a word, you will pronounce it and allow the Deaf person to lipread to supplement your fingerspelling.

Practice

Do not become discouraged if your movements are not as smooth as you wish at first. Practice is the key. The signed sentences in this book should be practiced a minimum of three times a week. Learning any language requires practice, and anyone who fails to practice will make little progress.

It has been estimated that there are approximately 28 million deaf and hard-of-hearing persons in the United States. The sign language skills you acquire through your study and practice can enable you to communicate with most of the Deaf people whom you may encounter.

May your study of sign language be a happy and rewarding experience.

Manual Alphabet

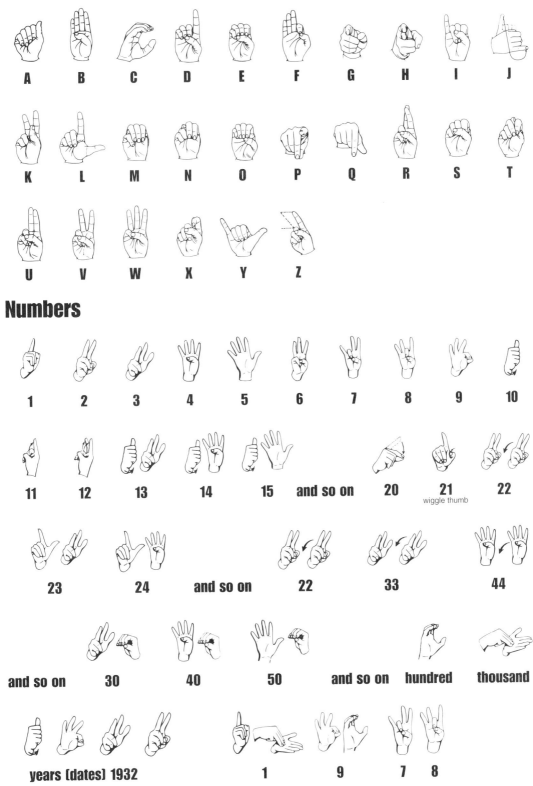

Numbers

American Manual Alphabet used by permission of Gallaudet University Press.

To sign double digit numbers with the same number, e.g., "22," sign "2," then move your hand slightly to the right to indicate the second digit.

22

Lesson 1

1. ✓ **Hello!**
like salute

✓ **Good-bye!**
2X

2. ✓ **How** **are** **you** **?**
BHA   F-X

3. ✓ **I** **am** **fine!**
R
[5 hand]

4. **Thank you.**
BHA / OUT

5. **You** **are** ✓ **welcome.**
R→B

6. ✓ **Excuse**
R-in-L / 2X
dismiss, pardon, forgive

✓ **me.**

7. **I** **am** ✓ **sorry.**
R-on-B
sorrow
[A over heart]

8. ✓ R-on-B
Please.
like, enjoy, privilege,
appreciate, pleasure

9. ✓
Are   **you**   **deaf** F-X **?**

10. ✓
Are   **you**   2X **hearing** F-X **?**
speaking

11. ✓
What

✓ R-on-L
time   **is**   **it** F-X **?**
wristwatch   now, presently

12. ✓
Today   **is**
now + day

✓ CW
Monday.

13. ✓
Tomorrow   **is**   CW **Tuesday.**

14. ✓
Yesterday   **was**   CW **Wednesday;**   **Thursday;**
Y - past

√ CW
Friday;

√ CW
Saturday;

√
Sunday.

15. BHA / AA   R→B
Come

√
with

me.

16.
It **is**

√ R-on-B
my
mine
[touch chest]

√ BHA
book.

17.
It **is**

√ R-on-B
mine.
my
[touch chest]

18.
I

√
will
shall, would

√ BHA / AA   OUT / →R
go
went
opposite of *come*

√ 2X
myself.

19. √ R-on-L
Practice
train

it **with** **me.**

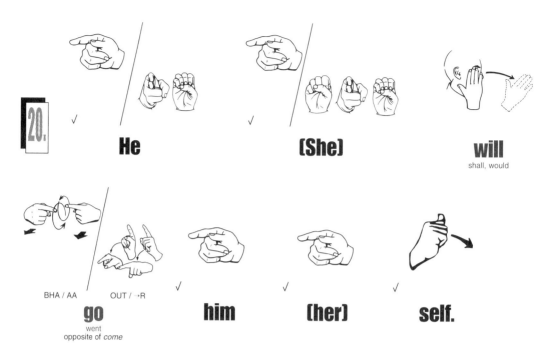

20. ✓ **He** ✓ **[She]** **will**
shall, would

BHA / AA OUT / →R

go ✓ **him** ✓ **[her]** ✓ **self.**
went
opposite of *come*

Fingerspelling Practice Drills

("at" words)

bat, cat, date, fat, fate, fatal, gate, ate, eat, hat, hate, late, Kate, mat, mate, cat, goat, pat, rate, rat, tat, vat, sat, sate, grate, crate, plate, state, slate, skate

1 2 3 4 5 6 7 8 9 10

Practice Sentences

1. He practiced with me Monday.
2. She came to thank him Tuesday.
3. Tomorrow is Wednesday.
4. She will go herself.
5. Friday was a fine day.
6. Excuse me, are you deaf or hearing?
7. What time is it please?
8. The book is mine.
9. I am pleased with you.
10. Practice the book with me.
11. Please come with me Thursday.
12. You are welcome to come with me Sunday.
13. Monday I will go myself.
14. She was sorry you came.
15. He will be pleased with the book.
16. Excuse me, will you go?
17. Yesterday he was fine.
18. He will go practice with me.
19. Tomorrow is Friday.
20. I will practice with you tomorrow.
21. Sunday I will go with her.
22. Yesterday I was sorry.
23. Please excuse me; it is my book.
24. Today you are welcome to go with me.

New Signs List

Word	Synonym	Memory Aid	Sentence	Word	Synonym	Memory Aid	Sentence
book	—	—	16	please	like, enjoy privilege, appreciate, pleasure	—	8
come	—	—	15	practice	train	—	19
deaf	—	—	9	Saturday	—	—	14
excuse	dismiss, pardon, forgive	—	6	self, himself, herself	—	—	20
fine	—	—	3	she	—	—	20
Friday	—	—	14	sorry	sorrow	—	7
go	went	opposite of *come*	18,20	Sunday	—	—	14
good-bye	—	—	1	thank you	—	—	4
he	—	—	20	Thursday	—	—	14
hearing	speaking	—	10	time	—	wristwatch	11
hello	—	like salute	1	today	—	*now + day*	12
him	—	—	20	tomorrow	—	—	13
how	—	—	2	Tuesday	—	—	13
I	—	—	3,7,18	Wednesday	—	—	14
it	now, presently	—	11	welcome	—	—	5
me	—	—	6.15.19	what	—	—	11
mine	my	—	17	will	shall, would	—	18,20
Monday	—	—	12	with	—	—	15,19
my	mine	—	16	yesterday	—	*Y - past*	14
myself	—	—	18	you	—	—	2,5,9,10

Lesson 2

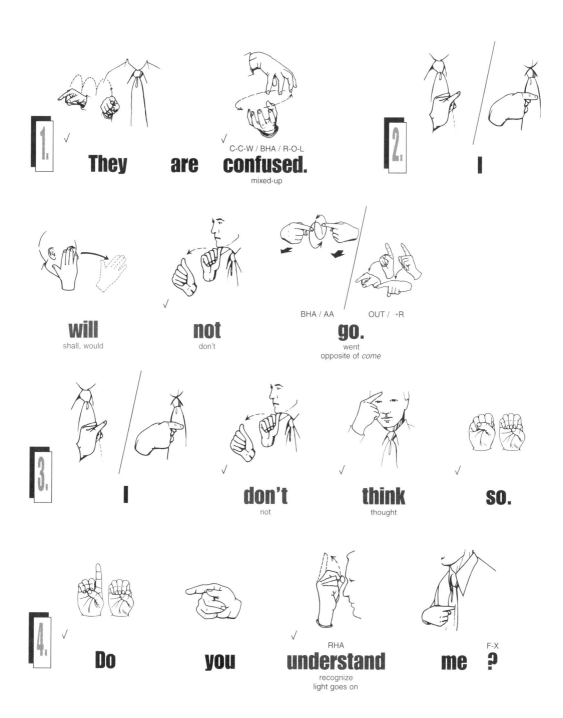

1. They are confused.
C-C-W / BHA / R-O-L
mixed-up

2. I

will
shall, would

not
don't

go.
BHA / AA · · · · OUT / ·R
went
opposite of *come*

3. I don't think so.
not · · · thought

4. Do you understand me ?
RHA · · · F-X
recognize
light goes on

5.

Do **you** **want** **something ?**

√ L→B 2X F-X

long for, desire,
wish

6.

√

Did **you** **go** **?**

BHA / AA OUT / →R F-X

went
opposite of *come*

7.

What **is** **this** **?**

√ F-X

now, here

8.

He

was **planning** **to** **go.**

√ √ [*P* hands] F →R BHA / AA OUT / →R

past, ago, preparing, arranging went
previous(ly) opposite of *come*

9.

He **is the** **past** **president.**

√ √ BHA

previously, ago superintendent

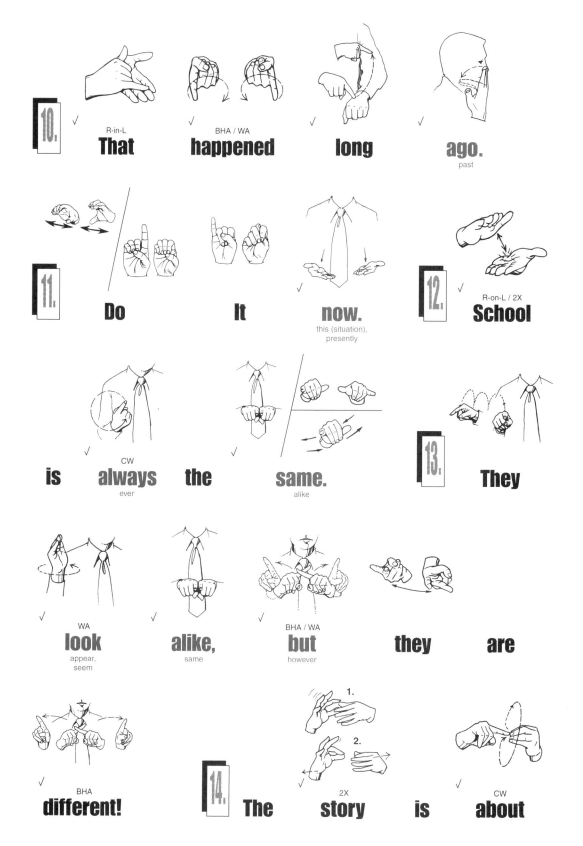

10. ✓

R-in-L
That

✓
BHA / WA
happened

✓
long

✓
ago.
past

11. ✓
Do

It

✓
now.
this (situation),
presently

12. ✓
R-on-L / 2X
School

✓
CW
is **always** **the**
ever

✓
same.
alike

13. ✓
They

✓
WA
look
appear,
seem

✓
alike,
same

✓
BHA / WA
but
however

they **are**

✓
BHA
different!

14. ✓
1.
2.
2X
The **story** **is**

✓
CW
about

John.

15. He went
BHA / AA   OUT / →R
go
opposite of *come*

to church.
R-on-L
[*C* hand]

16. Call the children
R-on-L   F →R
child
[pat heads of children]

from home.
RHA
eat + sleep

17. You are wanted
L →B
long for, desire,
wish

on the telephone.

18. She called
BHA
named

him Jack.

19. Introduce us!
RHA

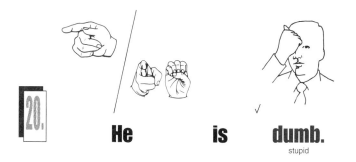

20. **He** **is** **dumb.**
stupid

Fingerspelling Practice Drills

("am" words)

bam, cam, dam, ream, fame, game, ham, jam, lam, lame, mama, exam, loam, foam, roam, ram, Sam, same, tam, tame, vamp

11 12 13 14 15 16 17 18 19 20

Practice Sentences

1. They are planning to go home now.
2. Are you going to church?
3. I think they are from the same school.
4. It happened a long time ago.
5. They confused the president.
6. The story is different.
7. Introduce us to the president.
8. John is not dumb, but he is confused.
9. How long did he understand this?
10. The past president was confused.
11. He went to children's church.
12. They look different, but they are alike.
13. John went to church.
14. I do not want to go.
15. The children look alike.
16. He is confused.
17. The story about the president was confusing.
18. I planned to introduce Jack to Mary.
19. They called the children.
20. I want to go to church.
21. He is always planning to do something.
22. What is the story?
23. She called John on the telephone.
24. He did not understand but was confused.

New Signs List

Word	Synonym	Memory Aid	Sentence	Word	Synonym	Memory Aid	Sentence
about	—	—	14	not	don't	—	2,3
ago	past	—	10	now	this, presently	—	11
alike	same	—	13	past	previously, ago	—	9
always	ever	—	12	planning	preparing, arranging	—	8
but	however	—	13	president	superinten-dent	—	9
call	—	—	16	same	alike	—	12
called	named	—	18	school	—	—	12
children	child	—	16	so	—	—	3
church	—	—	15	something	—	—	5
confused	—	mixed-up	1	story	—	—	14
did	—	—	6	telephone	—	—	17
different	—	—	13	that	—	—	10
do	—	—	4,5	they	—	—	1,13
don't	not	—	3	think	thought	—	3
dumb	stupid	—	20	this	now, here	—	7
from	—	—	16	to	—	—	15
happened	—	—	10	understand	recognize	light goes on	4
home	—	*eat* + sleep	16	us	—	—	19
introduce	—	—	19	want	long for, desire, wish	—	5,17
look	appear, seem	—	13	was	past, ago, previous(ly)	—	8
long	—	—	10	—	—	—	—

Lesson 3

1. BHA
How **do** **you** √ F→R / WF **spell** R-in-L **that**

√ **word** F-X **?**

2. **Do** **you** √ **like** R

√ BHA / EA / IN **sign** √ BHA / WA **language** F-X **?**

3. **Do** **you**

BHA / AA **go** OUT / →R
went
opposite of *come*

to **the** √ **Assemblies of God**

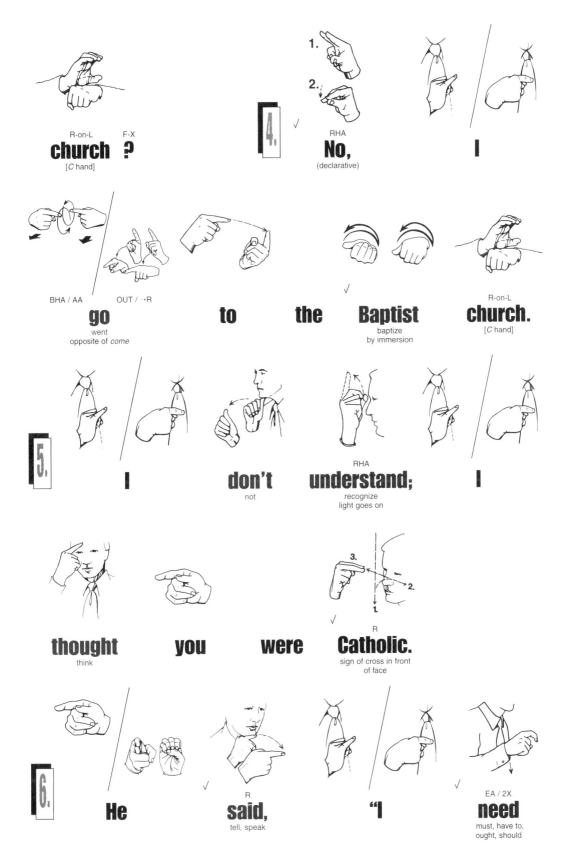

R-on-L   F-X
church ?
[*C* hand]

4. ✓

RHA
No,
(declarative)

I

BHA / AA   OUT / →R
go
went
opposite of *come*

to

the

✓
Baptist
baptize
by immersion

R-on-L
church.
[*C* hand]

5.

I

don't
not

RHA
understand;
recognize
light goes on

I

thought
think

you

were

✓
R
Catholic.
sign of cross in front
of face

6.

He

✓
R
said,
tell, speak

✓
"I

✓
EA / 2X
need
must, have to,
ought, should

to   talk   to   her!"

2X   BHA / AA

7. I   called   for   help.

R-on-L   WA   L-in-R

8. You   must   phone   me.

EA / 2X   call

need, have to, ought, should

9. Where   did   you   get

grab the rope

that   animal ?

R-in-L   BHA / 2X   F-X

10. That   is   my

R-in-L   R-on-B

mine
[touch chest]

✓ R-on-L / 2X
work.
labor, job

11.

You

EA / 2X
must
need, have to,
ought, should

✓ R-on-L
keep
[*K* hands]

R-in-L
that

✓ 2X
dog
snap fingers

at

RHA
home.
eat + sleep

12.

You

✓ EA / 2X
should
need, have to,
ought, must

BHA / AA
go
went
opposite of *come*

OUT / →R
to

✓ BHA
class.
[*C* hands]

13.

✓ **His**

✓ RHA / 2X
experience
gray hair showing wisdom

✓ R-in-L
in

✓ BHA / 2X
football
scrimmage

is

✓ BHA / WA / R-O-L
limited.
maximum & minimum
cutoff

14.

He

is

✓ BHA
very

✓

RHA / WA

experienced
skilled, adept

R-in-L

in

his

✓

R-in-L / 2X

job.
work, labor

15.

It

is

a

✓

R-on-L

nice
clean

✓

RHA

day.

16.

I

will
shall, would

✓

BHA

meet
[bump into each other]

you

✓

R-in-L

at
(time)
wristwatch

✓

noon.
[sun directly overhead]

17.

R

Tell
say, speak

me

✓

R-in-L

again

CW

about

✓

OUT

your
(possessive)

✓

WA / 2X

cat.
whiskers

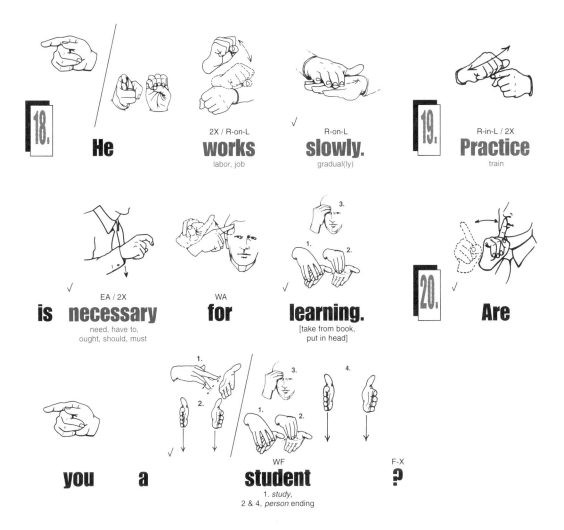

He **works** / **slowly.** **Practice**
labor, job / gradual(ly) / train
2X / R-on-L / R-on-L / R-in-L / 2X

is **necessary** **for** **learning.** **Are**
need, have to, / WA / [take from book,
ought, should, must / put in head]
EA / 2X

you **a** **student** **?**
WF / F-X
1. *study*,
2 & 4, *person* ending

Fingerspelling Practice Drills
("th" words)

that, the, this, there, they, then, them, those, throw, throne, thrice, thrown, Thursday, think, thank, than, thaw, three, their, threw, thick, thin, thief, thigh, thrift, thirst, thong, thorn, thing, thread, threat, three, thresh, thirst, throb, throng, thumb, thwart, thyme, thus, with

21 22 23 24 25 26 27 28 29 30

Practice Sentences

1. Where do you go to church?
2. You must limit your football practice.
3. It is necessary for students to go to class.
4. How did you get that job?
5. Do you like the Assemblies of God church?
6. Your dog is at the Baptist church.
7. I need you to spell that word for me again.
8. I don't understand, where is your cat?
9. You must practice to get experienced.
10. I need to talk to her about her dog.
11. You should go to the Catholic church.
12. You must phone me about football Tuesday.
13. That student likes sign language.
14. I need to phone home.
15. I will meet you in class.
16. Is that animal a cat?
17. Phone me today about going to practice.
18. Help me practice football.
19. It is necessary for a student to learn.
20. Football practice is at the Baptist church.
21. We are learning sign language today.
22. Do you understand the book about animals?
23. The Baptist and Catholic church are different.
24. Friday I will come with the Deaf.

New Signs List

Word	Synonym	Memory Aid	Sentence	Word	Synonym	Memory Aid	Sentence
a	—	—	15	meet	—	—	16
again	—	—	17	must	have to, ought, should, need	—	8,11
animal	—	—	9	necessary	need, must, should, ought, have to	—	19
Assemblies of God	—	—	3	need	must, have to, ought, should	—	6
at	—	wristwatch	16	nice	clean	—	15
Baptist	baptize	by immersion	4	no	—	—	4
cat	—	whiskers	17	noon	—	—	16
Catholic	—	sign of cross	5	*person* ending	—	—	20
class	—	—	12	phone	call	—	8
day	—	—	15	said	tell, speak	—	6
dog	—	snap fingers	11	said	tell, speak	—	6
experience	—	gray hair of wisdom	13	should	must, need, have to, ought	—	12
experienced	skilled, adept	—	14	sign	—	—	2
football	—	scrimmage	13	slowly	gradual(ly)	—	18
for	—	—	7,19	spell	—	—	1
get	—	grab the rope	9	student	—	1. *study*, 2. person ending	20
help	—	—	7	talk	—	—	6
his	—	—	13,14	tell	say, speak	—	17
in	—	—	13,14	very	—	—	14
job	work, labor	—	14	where	—	—	9
keep	—	—	11	word	—	—	1
language	—	—	2	work	labor, job	—	10,18
learning	—	—	19	your	—	—	17
limited	—	maximum & minimum cutoff	13	—	—	—	—

Lesson 4

1.

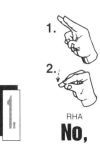

RHA
No,
(declarative)

I

am

a

√
BHA / 2X
teacher.

2.

√
We

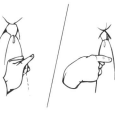

BHA / AA   OUT / →R
go
went
opposite of come

to

the

same
alike

R-on-L / 2X
school

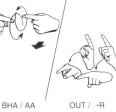

√
R-on-L
(college,
school + over

√
R-on-L
university).
[R U]

3.

What

is

the

√
R-on-L
name

of

R-in-L
that

BHA
book

you   **are**   **reading ?**
F-X
eyes scanning book

4.   **Please**
R-on-B
like, enjoy, privilege,
appreciate, pleasure

write
R-in-L

a   **letter**
R-in-L
affix stamp
on envelope

for
WA

me.

5.   **She**   **is**   **the**   **president's**   **secretary.**
R-in-L
take pencil from
behind ear + write

6.   **The**   **lesson**
R-on-L
sermon, message,
course, subject

showed
example

good
R-in-L

planning.
F→R
preparing, arranging
[*P* hands]

7.   **Bring**
L→R
carry

me

some
R-in-L
part, a portion

paper.
R-on-L / 2X

8.

He

phones
calls

me

√ R-in-L / 2X
often
again & *again*

CW
about

his

√ BHA / AA
troubles.
trials, cares

9.

We

√ R-in-L
all

BHA / OUT
thank you

WA
for

your
(possessive)

L-in-R
help.

10.

Do

you

√ **have**
(possessive)

a

√ L-on-R F-X
turtle ?

11.

RHA
No,
(declarative)

BHA / WA
but
however

I

do

have **a** ✓ RHA **frog.**
(possessive)

12. R-on-B **My** ✓ **friend**
mine
[touch chest]
hooked forefingers

✓ **has** **a** ✓ 2X **squirrel** ✓ F→R **too.** **13.** **The**
(possessive)
also

R-on-L **church** EA / 2X **needs** ✓ **men** ✓ **who** C-C-W
[C hand]
must, have to,
ought, should

✓ **are** R **true** ✓ AA / BHA **servants.** **14.** R-in-L **That**
sure
[up and out from mouth]

✓ 2X **boy** **is** **his** ✓ **son.**
male + small
male + cradled in arms

15. **The** **girl** **walking** **with** **him**

female + *small* / 2X / BHA / AA / steps

is **six** **years** **old.** **16.** **Which**

age / beard [*O* hand] / BHA / AA / which one, whether

person **do** **you** **prefer** **best** **?**

personal / [*P* hands] / rather / F-X

17. **When** **did** **he** **leave** **?**

RHA / BHA / L→B / F-X / left, depart

18. **They** **live** **together.** **19.** **People**

C-C-W / BHA / with, circled / BHA / IN / EA / AA / [*P* hands]

came — R →B / BHA / AA ✓

from ✓

far ✓

and — RHA / L →R ✓

near ✓
close

to

hear ✓
listen
C at R ear

him.

20.

Did

you

remember ✓
stay in mind

to

bring — L →R
carry

your
(possessive)

eight - ✓

page ✓
2X
turn page

book F-X
?

Fingerspelling Practice Drills
("oa" words)

boat, coat, road, goat, load, goad, float, throat, Noah, loam, foal, toad, loamy, moat, gloat, goal, roan, soak, loan

31 32 33 34 35 36 37 38 39 40

Practice Sentences

1. The secretary showed good planning.
2. She is reading his eight-page letter.
3. Do you remember the lesson from church?
4. The student went to college with that book.
5. The president was planning for the lesson.
6. What are the names of your turtle and frog?
7. That six-year-old boy has a squirrel.
8. Write a letter for me.
9. My teacher has a good friend with a turtle.
10. He often has troubles.
11. What is the name of that college?
12. The teacher showed me the reading book.
13. He often has troubles at the university.
14. When did they go to church together?
15. Which university do you prefer?
16. Please bring me the president's book.
17. The president is a teacher at this college.
18. Thank you for planning the lesson.
19. Do you remember what he came to tell you?
20. The president often calls me about his frog.
21. People come from far and near for church.
22. They have eight squirrels that live together.
23. All the people are very old.
24. Please remember to help people in need.

New Signs List

Word	Synonym	Memory Aid	Sentence	Word	Synonym	Memory Aid	Sentence
all	—	—	9	people	—	—	19
and	—	—	19	person	personal	—	16
best	—	—	16	prefer	rather	—	16
boy	—	*male + small*	14	president's	—	—	5
bring	carry	—	7,20	reading	—	eyes scanning book	3
came	—	—	19	remember	—	stay in mind	20
college	—	*school + over*	2	secretary	—	take pencil from behind ear + write	5
eight	—	—	20	servants	—	—	13
far	—	—	19	showed	example	—	6
friend	—	hooked forefingers	12	six	—	—	15
frog	—	—	11	some	part, portion	—	7
girl	—	*female + small*	15	son	—	male + cradle in arms	14
good	—	—	6	squirrel	—	—	12
has (poss.)	—	—	12	teacher	—	—	1
have (poss.)	—	—	10,11	together	—	*with*, circled	18
hear	listen	*C* at R ear	19	too	also	—	12
leave	left, depart	—	17	troubles	trials, cares	—	8
lesson	sermon, message, course, subject	—	6	true	sure	—	13
letter	—	affix stamp on envelope	4	turtle	—	—	10
live	—	—	18	university	—	—	2
men	man, male	—	13	walking	—	steps	15
name	—	—	3	we	—	—	2
near	close	—	19	when	—	—	17
often	—	*again* & *again*	8	which	which one, whether	—	16
old	age	beard	15	who	whom	—	13
page	—	turn page	20	write	—	—	4
paper	—	—	7	years	—	—	15

Lesson 5

1. ✓ **Why** [*Y* hand]   ✓ **didn't** ^R don't, not   **you**   **call** R-on-L   **me**   **?** F-X

2. ✓ **Most** RHA   **of**   **us**   **wanted** L→B long for, desire, wish   **to**

go. BHA / AA   OUT / →R went opposite of *come*

3. **We**   **always** CW ever

go BHA / AA   OUT / →R went opposite of *come*   ✓ **to** →R   **Sunday school.** Sunday + school

4.

We ✓ **never** ✓ **miss**
absent

a **church**
R-on-L
[*C* hand]

✓ **service.**
meeting, gathering

5. **How**
BHA

✓ **could**
can, able,
power

you

✓ **forget**
RHA
wipe from mind

that
R-in-L

?
F-X

6. **Did** **you**

✓ **know**
known, knowledge,
aware, conscious

he **is**

✓ **Jewish**
2X
goatee

?
F-X

7. **I** **thought**
think

he **came**
R→B / BHA / AA

from

Germany.
R-on-L / WF

8.

He **is**

running
→R   R-U-L / 2X

fast.
R
quick, sudden, immediate
shoot marbles

9.

Do **you**

have
(possessive)

any
WA / →R
[A hand]

money ?
R-in-L / 2X   F-X

10.

Did

you

buy
R-in-L
purchase
money paid out

your
(possessive)

sign
BHA / EA / IN

language
BHA / WA

book ?
BHA   F-X

11.

I

told
R
say, speak

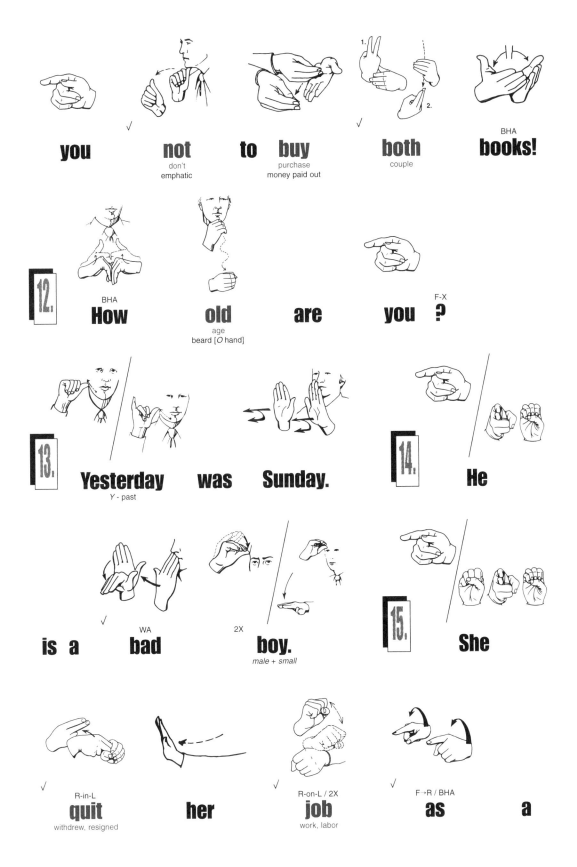

you

not
don't
emphatic

to

buy
purchase
money paid out

both
couple

BHA
books!

12.

BHA
How

old
age
beard [*O* hand]

are

you

F-X
?

13.

Yesterday
Y - past

was

Sunday.

14.

He

is a

WA
bad

2X
boy.
male + small

15.

She

quit
R-in-L
withdrew, resigned

her

job
R-on-L / 2X
work, labor

as
F→R / BHA

a

a **secretary.**
R-in-L
take pencil from
behind ear + write

16.

She **is** **happy** **to be**
√
2X
glad, rejoice

home.
RHA
eat + sleep

17.

The **news**
√
R-in-L
new

made
√
R-on-L
make

me

sad.
√
long face

18.

Let's
√
WA
allow, may

go
BHA / AA   OUT / →R
went
opposite of *come*

out!
√
[L *C* hand]

19.

He

arrived
√
R-in-L

late
√
not yet, yet

for
WA

class.
BHA
[*C* hands]

20.

He

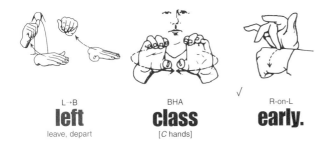

L→B	BHA	√ R-on-L
left	**class**	**early.**
leave, depart	[*C* hands]	

Fingerspelling Practice Drills

("ea" words)

beat, cease, grease, gear, heat, heal, jeans, yéarn, beam, meal, hear, heap, leap, mean, meant, peal, near, zeal, lean, weak, deal, seam, pea, ream, lead, reap, dream, steam, seal, seat, real, scream, team, dead, eat, feat, veal, tease, gleam, steam

41 42 43 44 45 46 47 48 49 50

Practice Sentences

1. Did you miss the Sunday school service?
2. We wanted to go to Germany Sunday.
3. I came to class early yesterday.
4. The secretary quit.
5. The news made me leave class early.
6. How could you forget?
7. He is running fast to get the turtle.
8. The news makes me sad.
9. The secretary arrived late for work.
10. Yesterday she arrived home from Germany.
11. Why didn't you call me?
12. She got the sad news from home.
13. I told you never to miss a church service.
14. He forgot that you came from Germany.
15. When did the Jewish girl leave?
16. Bring that letter to church for me.
17. She is happy that her son goes to church.
18. The Jew forgot his sign language book.
19. Don't forget to go to church.
20. He arrived at his job late, so he quit.
21. The old person was late for class.
22. Did you quit your job today?
23. Most Jews were sad in Germany.
24. We arrived late for Sunday school today.

New Signs List

Word	Synonym	Memory Aid	Sentence	Word	Synonym	Memory Aid	Sentence
any	—	—	9	let's	allow, may	—	18
arrived	—	—	19	made	make	—	17
as	—	—	15	miss	absent	—	4
bad	—	—	14	money	—	—	9
both	couple	—	11	most	—	—	2
buy	purchase	money paid out	10,11	never	—	—	4
could	can, able, power	—	5	news	new	—	17
didn't	don't, not	—	1	not	don't	emphatic	11
early	—	—	20	out	—	—	18
fast	quick, sudden, immediate	shoot marbles	8	quit	withdraw, resign	—	15
forget	—	wipe from mind		running	—	—	8
Germany	—	—	7	sad	—	long face	17
happy	glad, rejoice	—	16	service	meeting, gathering	—	4
her (possessive)	—	—	15	Sunday school	—	—	3
Jewish	—	goatee	6	told	say, speak	—	11
know	known, knowledge, aware, conscious	—	6	why	—	—	1
late	not yet, yet	—	19	—	—	—	—

Lesson 6

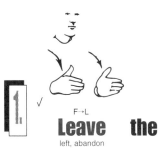  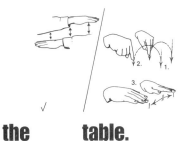

1.

√

F→L
Leave   the   **book**   **on**   the   **table.**

left, abandon

BHA

R-on-L

rest arm on table / 4 legs and a top

2.

Did   **you**   **hear**   the   **story**

listen
[C at R ear]

2X

 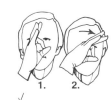   

CW
about   the   **fox**   **and**   the   **elephant** ?

√

RHA / L→R

√

F-X

trunk of elephant

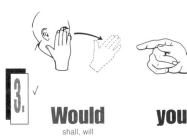 

3.

√

Would   **you**   **please**   √ **finish**   **that**

shall, will

R-on-B
like, enjoy, privilege,
appreciate, pleasure

complete, already

R-in-L

job ?
R-on-L / 2X   F-X
work, labor

4.

I

already
finish

did
do

that!
R-in-L

5.

Flowers
R ›L
smell

bloom

in
R-in-L

the

spring.
R-in-L /2X
grow

6.

Did

you

have
(possessive)

a

nice
R-on-L
clean

summer
L ›R
wipe perspiration

vacation ?
WF   F-X
idle

7.

School
R-on-L / 2X

[College]
R-on-L
school + over

begins
R-in-L / WA
starts, instituted,
initially

in
R-in-L

the

fall.
2X
leaves falling

8. **Winters** **in** **Missouri** **are** **much**
cold
R-in-L
a lot of, amount
[large quantity]

warmer **than** **in** **the** **north**
R-on-L
R-in-L
[same directions as
when facing map]

(south, **east,** **west).** **9.** **They**

were **married** **during** **the** **summer.**
in past,
previously
while
L→R
wipe perspiration

10. **I** **have** **one** **son**
(possessive)
male + cradled in arms

and

RHA / L→R

one

daughter.
female + cradled in arms

11.

I

have
(possessive)

three

brothers
male + *same*

and
RHA / L→R

one

sister.
female + *same*

12.

They

are

now
this, here

husband
male + *married*

and
RHA / L→R

wife.
female + *married*

13.

He

is

a

Methodist
BHA / AA
eager, enthusiastic,
ambitious

preacher.
R / 2X

14. He / is — saving ✓ / R-on-L / storing, reserving — his — money / R-in-L / 2X

for / WA — a — trip ✓ / R / OUT / travel, journey — to — Europe. ✓ / C-C-W / [E toward face]

15. He — plans / F→R / prepares, arranges / [P hands] — to — visit ✓ / OUT / BHA / AA / [V hands] — England, ✓ / R-on-L / English

Ireland, ✓ / R-on-L / potato — Holland, ✓ / [Y like pipe] — and / RHA / L→R — Italy. ✓ / Italian / [I like Catholic]

16. I — want / L→B / long for, desire, wish — to — have / (possessive) — turkey, ✓

√
chicken,
bird

or

√
duck

WA
for

√
Thanksgiving

1.
2.
1.
√
2X
dinner.
lunch
eat + noon

17.
I

will
shall, would

BHA
meet

you

at

1.
1.
2.
2X
dinner.
lunch
eat + noon

18.
I

know
known, knowledge,
aware, conscious

it

√
BHA
used to be
in the past

√
C-C-W
around

√
here.

19.
Why
[Y hand]

R
don't
didn't, not

you **ask** **him** **to** **review** **it** **?**

F→B
pray

F-X

look back

Please **put** **away** **your** **science**

R-on-B

like, enjoy, privilege,
appreciate, pleasure

F→R
place

→R

(possessive)

BHA / AA
pour test
tubes

20.

books **and** **magazines.**

BHA / 2X

RHA / L→R

2X

Fingerspelling Practice Drills

("an" words)

any, ant, ban, can, Dan, Jan, fan, man, pan, ran, tan, van, hand, Jane, land, many, loan, pant, rant, sand, sank, want, Anna, Danny, Annas, gander, handle, Cantor, landed, tanned, wander, Andrew, Daniel

51 52 53 54 55 56 57 58 59 60

Practice Sentences

1. I want to meet your daughter in Europe.
2. He is the preacher for the Methodist church.
3. I will buy an elephant for my brother.
4. The flowers in Ireland are blooming early.
5. My husband's job was to be a preacher.
6. I have two brothers and one sister.
7. I thought Holland used to be around here.
8. Do flowers bloom in the winter?
9. There is an elephant in the flowers.
10. Ducks in Ireland are saved for dinner.
11. It was warm on our vacation.
12. Please finish that book you are reading.
13. Would you please finish reading the story.
14. They were married in Italy in the summer.
15. He is saving his money.
16. I have brothers who live in Missouri.
17. The table I use comes from Italy.
18. The preacher plans to visit Ireland.
19. My son and his wife had a nice vacation.
20. The flowers on the table are for the elephant.
21. You could go north for your vacation.
22. He wanted my money for Holland.
23. His daughter was married in the spring.
24. Did you finish the chicken for dinner?

New Signs List

Word	Synonym	Memory Aid	Sentence	Word	Synonym	Memory Aid	Sentence
already	finish	—	4	Missouri	—	MO	8
around	—	—	18	much, large	a lot of, amount	—	8
ask	pray	—	19	north	—	—	8
away	—	—	20	one	—	—	10,11
begins	starts, instituted, initially	—	7	preacher	—	—	13
bloom	—	—	5	put	place	—	20
brothers	—	male + same	11	review	—	look back	19
chicken	bird	—	16	saving	storing, reserving	—	14
daughter	—	female + cradled in arms	10	science	—	pour test tubes	20
did	do	—	4	sister	—	female + same	11
dinner	lunch	eat + noon	16,17	south	—	—	8
duck	—	—	16	spring	grow	—	5
during	while	—	9	summer	—	wipe perspiration	6,9
east	—	—	8	table	—	4 legs and a top, rest arms	1
elephant	—	trunk of elephant	2	than	—	—	8
England	English	—	15	Thanksgiving	—	—	16
Europe	—	—	14	three	—	—	11
fall (season)	—	leaves falling	7	trip	travel, journey	—	14
finish	already, complete	—	3	turkey	—	—	16
flowers	—	smell	5	used to be	in the past	—	18
fox	—	—	2	vacation	idle	—	6
here	—	—	18	visit	—	—	15
Holland	—	Y like pipe	15	warmer	—	—	8
husband	—	male + married	12	were	previously, in past	—	9
Ireland	potato	—	15	west	—	facing map	8
Italy	Italian	—	15	wife	—	female + married	12
leave	left, abandon	—	1	winters	cold	—	8
magazines	—	—	20	would	shall, will		3
married	—	—	9	—	—	—	
Methodist	eager, enthusiastic, ambitious	—	13	—	—	—	

Lesson 7

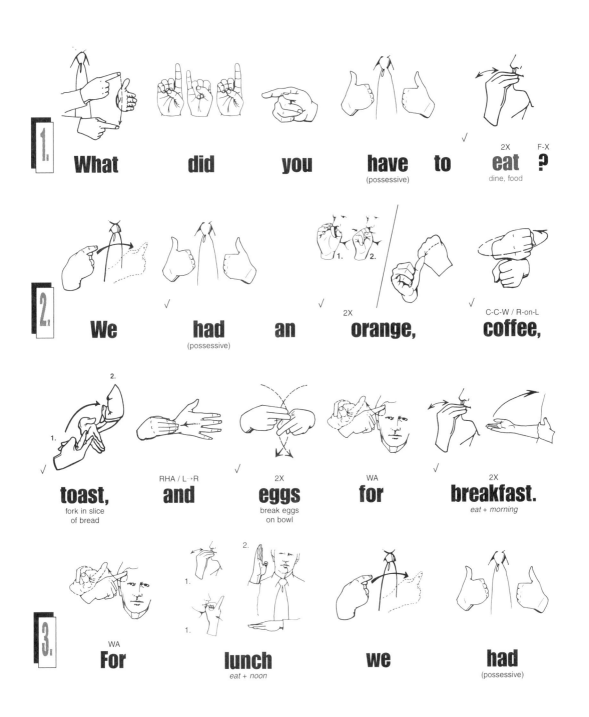

1.

What   **did**   **you**   **have** **to**   **eat** **?**

(possessive)   2X   F-X
                   dine, food

2.

We   **had**   **an**   **orange,**   **coffee,**

(possessive)   2X   C-C-W / R-on-L

toast,   **and**   **eggs**   **for**   **breakfast.**

fork in slice   RHA / L→R   2X   WA   2X
of bread   break eggs   *eat + morning*
                   on bowl

3.

   WA
For   **lunch**   **we**   **had**

       eat + noon   (possessive)

R-on-L	√ WA / R	√	√	RHA / L→R
potatoes,	**onions,**	**tomatoes,**	**meat,**	**and**
Ireland			flesh	

√ 2X	4.			R
ice cream.	**Do**	**you**	**like**	
eating cone				

√ RUL / 2X	R-on-L		R-on-L F-X
gravy	**on**	**your**	**potatoes ?**
oil		(possessive)	Ireland

5.	**I**	√ R	√ 2X	√ R-on-L / 2X
		like	**crackers,**	**cheese,**
				pivot palms

RHA / L→R	√ R-in-L / WA	6.	√ R
and	**tea.**	**He**	**is**	**feeling**
	tea bag in cup		

much
a lot of, amount
[comparative or quantity]

better

today.
now + day

That
R-in-L

is   **a**   **large**
great, big

book
BHA

you

are

carrying.
bringing
L ·R

Do

you

think
thought

you

can
could, able,
power

swallow

it   **?**
F-X

Yesterday
Y - past

Mary

ran
·L   R-U-L / 2X

around
C-C-W

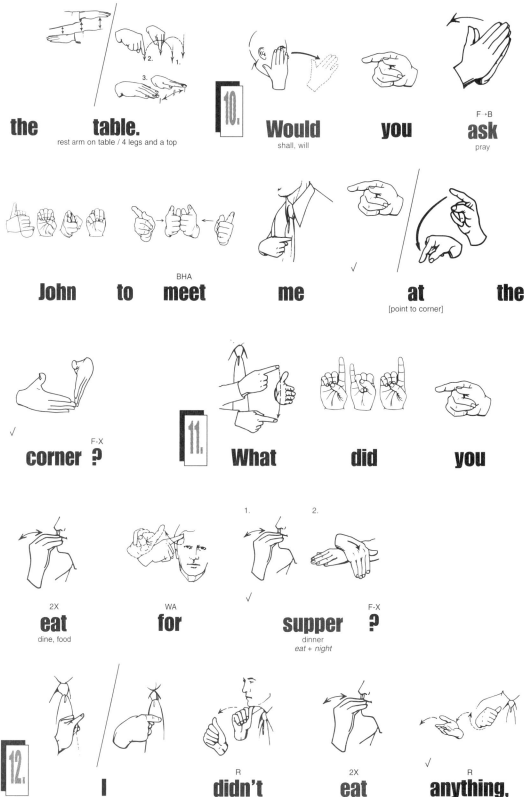

the   **table.**

rest arm on table / 4 legs and a top

10.   **Would**

shall, will

you   **ask**

F→B

pray

John   **to**   BHA **meet**   **me**   √ **at**   **the**

[point to corner]

√ **corner** F-X **?**   **11.**   **What**   **did**   **you**

2X **eat**

dine, food

WA **for**

√ **supper** F-X **?**

dinner
eat + night

12.   **I**   R **didn't**

don't, not

2X **eat**

dine, food

√ R **anything,**

BHA / WA
but
however

I

✓
WA
drank
drink

R-in-L
some
part

C-C-W / R-on-L
coffee.

13.

R-on-B
My
mine
[touch chest]

✓
father

RHA / L ·R
and

✓
mother

BHA / AA
are

OUT / ·R
going
went
opposite of *come*

·R
away.

14.
You

BHA / EA / IN
sign

better

now
here,
this

R-on-L
than

you

did

✓
R-O-L
before

you

BHA / AA
R ·B
came.

15.

He   **is**   **my**
R-on-B
mine
[touch chest]

best

friend.
hooked forefingers

16.

You   **should**
EA / 2X
need, have to,
ought, must

sign
BHA / EA / IN

large
great, big

when
RHA   BHA

in   **a**   **classroom.**
R-in-L   C + R (walls)

17.

She

√ **saw**
see

a

√ **deer**
antlers

√ **while**
during

√ **returning**
BHA / AA / IN
come + again

home
RHA
eat + sleep

from

√ **ice skating.**
BHA / AA

18.

Will
shall, would

you

R-on-L
keep
[*V* hands]

your
(possessive)

WA / 2X
cat
whiskers

at
[point toward home]

RHA   F-X
home ?
eat + sleep

19.

Can
could, able,
power

you

✓ R-on-L / IN
loan

me

R-in-L
some
example

R-in-L / 2X   F-X
money ?

20.

R-on-B
My
mine
[touch chest]

father

✓ R-on-L
borrowed
[*V* hands in]

R-in-L
all

the

R-in-L / 2X
money

he

EA / 2X
needed
must, have to,
ought, should

to

R-in-L
buy
purchase
money paid out

a

✓ BHA
house.
building

Fingerspelling Practice Drills

("is" words)

gist, hiss, list, miss, Lois, rise, mist, heist, anise, Louis, vista, sister, biscuit, Priscilla

61 62 63 64 65 66 67 68 69 70

Practice Sentences

1. Mary can swallow gravy while running.
2. Please carry your crackers and cheese.
3. I will visit my father when I go to Europe .
4. My six-year-old brother plays football.
5. I saw a deer at the Catholic church.
6. Last fall I went to Ireland for my vacation.
7. Put the book on the table.
8. Do you want to eat onions, eggs, and coffee?
9. She enjoys crackers and cheese for breakfast.
10. Would you like to borrow some tea?
11. My best friend came home from Germany.
12. Yesterday my cat ate potatoes and gravy.
13. Where do you go to church?
14. Put your money on the table.
15. He has experience working with elephants.
16. I am confused about what the teacher said.
17. Meet me in the classroom for ice cream.
18. Do you think she is happy with her job?
19. Did John have meat, toast, and an orange?
20. My sister is two years old.
21. Could you loan me some money for lunch?
22. Do you go to a college or university?
23. Please write a letter for me.
24. You need to make a lesson for the people.

New Signs List

Word	Synonym	Memory Aid	Sentence	Word	Synonym	Memory Aid	Sentence
anything	—	—	12	house	building	—	20
at (location)	—	—	10	ice cream	—	eating cone	3
before (point in time)	—	—	14	ice skating	—	—	17
better	—	—	6,14	large	great, big	—	7
borrowed	—	—	20	loan	—	—	19
breakfast	—	eat + morning	2	Mary	—	—	9
cheese	—	pivot palms	5	meat	flesh	—	3
classroom	—	C + R (walls)	16	mother	—	—	13
coffee	—	—	2,12	onions	—	—	3
corner	—	—	10	orange	—	—	2
crackers	—	—	5	ran	—	—	9
deer	—	antlers	17	returning	—	come + again	17
drank	drink	—	12	saw	see	—	17
eat	dine, food	—	1,11,12	supper	dinner	eat + night	11
eggs	—	break eggs on bowl	2	swallow	—	—	8
father	—	—	13,20	tea	—	tea bag in cup	5
feeling	—	—	6	toast	—	fork in slice of bread	2
gravy	oil	—	4	tomatoes	—	—	3
had	—	—	2	—	—	—	—

Lesson 8

1. ✓ The **law**
R-in-L

says
R
tell, speak

he

must
EA / 2X
need, have to,
ought, should

✓ **pay**
WA / R-in-L

eight ✓

percent ✓

interest.

2. **My**
R-on-B
mine
[touch chest]

✓ **aunt**
WA / 2X
A female

and
RHA / L→R

✓ **uncle**
WA / 2X
U male

✓ **have**
(completed action)

saved
R-on-L
store, reserve

✓ **enough**
R-on-L / OUT / 2X
sufficient

money
R-in-L / 2X

for
WA

✓ **their**

vacation.
WF
idle

3.

R-on-B
My
mine
[touch chest]

✓
WA / 2X
cousin
[*C* hand]

lives

R-in-L
in

✓
Michigan.
MI

4.

I

✓
have
(possessive)

✓
twelve
[palm toward body]

WA / 2X
nieces
N female

RHA / L→R
and

✓
WA / 2X
nephews.
N male

5.

Both
couple

R-on-B
my
mine
[touch chest]

✓
grandmother

RHA / L→R
and

✓
grandfather

are

✓
F→R
dead.
death
turn over

6.

I

R-on-B
enjoy
like, please, privilege,
appreciate, pleasure

a

✓
salad

made
make
R-on-L

with

√ **grapes,**
R-on-L

√ **pears,**
fruit + stem

and
RHA / L→R

√ **peaches.**
"peach fuzz" on face
2X

7. His

nephew is a Quaker.
WA / 2X
N male
BHA
twiddle thumbs

8. He

came
BHA / AA
R→B

here

from

√ **France.**
→R / WA
[*F*]

9. My
mine
[touch chest]
R-on-B

√ **neighbor**
near person

is a

close
near

friend
hooked forefingers

of

mine.
my
[touch chest]
R-on-B

10.

I   **make**   **it**   **a**   **habit**   **never**

R-on-L
made   mind + bound   CW

to   **have**   **any**   **enemies.**

(possessive)   →R   opposite person
            [A hand]

11.

Yesterday   **was**   **a**   **beautiful**   **day.**

Y - past   C-C-W   RHA
                            pretty, lovely,
                            beauty

12.

I   **think**   **the**   **picture**   **is**   **ugly.**

        thought   [C hand]   BHA
                                  grotesque
                                  [in front of face]

13.

He   **is**   **a**   **real**   **gentleman**   **and**

                       [R hand]   man + ruffles   RHA / L→R

his

wife
female + married

a

R
fine
[*5* hand]

lady.
woman + ruffles

14.

Their

parents
P chin, forehead

BHA / AA   R→B
came

from

Canada.
[grasp coat lapel]
2X

15.

They

both
couple

BHA / AA   R→B
come
opposite of *go*

from

good
R-in-L

families.
F + *class*
BHA

16.

I

understand
recognize
light goes on
RHA

that

she

was

their

only
alone, someone
C-C-W / EA

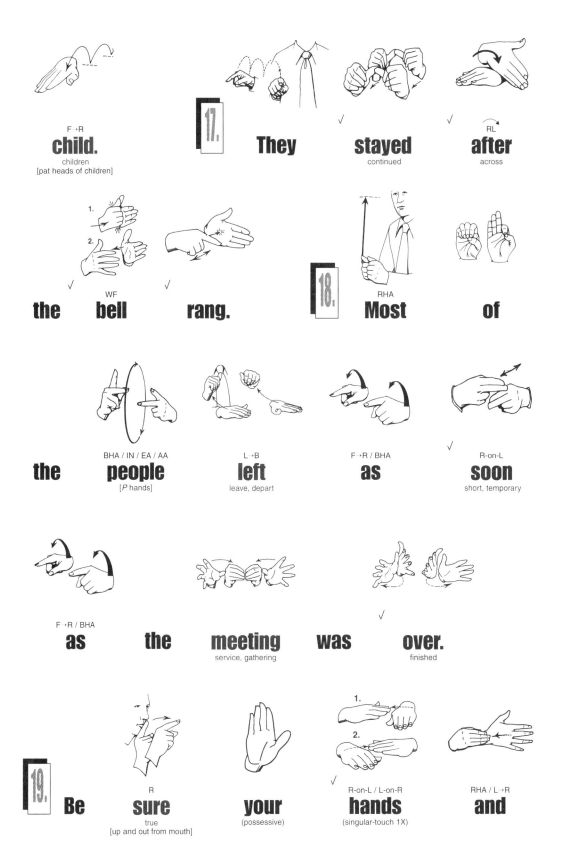

F→R
child.
children
[pat heads of children]

17.

They

✓
stayed
continued

✓
RL
after
across

1.
2.
✓
the

WF
bell

✓
rang.

18.

RHA
Most

of

the

BHA / IN / EA / AA
people
[P hands]

L→B
left
leave, depart

F→R / BHA
as

✓
R-on-L
soon
short, temporary

F→R / BHA
as

the

meeting
service, gathering

was

✓
over.
finished

19.

Be

R
sure
true
[up and out from mouth]

your
(possessive)

1.
2.
✓
R-on-L / L-on-R
hands
(singular-touch 1X)

RHA / L→R
and

C-C-W		R-on-L			
face	**are**	**clean.**		**Last**	
		nice		past, ago	

R-on-L		L→R		WF
week	**your**	**feet**	**were**	**dirty.**
	(possessive)			

Fingerspelling Practice Drills
("er" words)

aero, herd, mere, seer, very, veer, leer, deer, berry, Certs, eerie, Jerry, German, butler, period, career, lawyer

71 72 73 74 75 76 77 78 79 80

Practice Sentences

1. My cousins came to my house.
2. I want oranges and toast for breakfast.
3. My neighbor is my enemy.
4. I understand your face was dirty.
5. My preacher from Canada died.
6. My family enjoys eating grapes and peaches.
7. The lady and gentleman went to England.
8. My uncle says he left for Michigan last week.
9. Paul came here from France.
10. My parents make it a habit to visit Canada.
11. John must pay twenty-three percent interest.
12. She brought grapes, tomatoes, and cheese.
13. My aunt has two daughters-in-law.
14. Meet me for some ice cream after class.
15. Will you sign for my best friend?
16. We sure have a large classroom.
17. The boy is returning from Canada.
18. Are you saving for a trip to France?
19. My grandfather and grandmother are Quakers.
20. Her niece likes pears.
21. The boy ran as fast as the fox and the dog.
22. We had eggs and toast for breakfast.
23. The story about the old man was true.
24. You must finish your work.

New Signs List

Word	Synonym	Memory Aid	Sentence	Word	Synonym	Memory Aid	Sentence
after	across	—	17	law	—	—	1
aunt	—	*A* female	2	Michigan	—	*MI*	3
beautiful	pretty, lovely, beauty	—	11	neighbor	—	*near* person	9
bell	—	—	17	nephews	—	*N* male	4,7
Canada	—	—	14	nieces	—	*N* female	4
cousin	—	—	3	only	alone, someone	—	16
dead	death	turn over	5	over	finished	—	18
dirty	—	—	20	parents	—	*P* chin, forehead	14
enemies	—	*opposite* person	10	pay	—	—	1
enough	sufficient	—	2	peaches	—	"peach fuzz" on face	6
face	—	—	19	pears	—	fruit + stem	6
families	—	*F* + *class*	15	percent	—	—	1
feet	—	—	20	picture	—	*C* hand	12
France	—	—	8	Quaker	—	twiddle thumbs	7
gentleman	—	*man* + ruffles	13	rang	—	—	17
grandfather	—	—	5	real	—	—	13
grandmother	—	—	5	salad	—	—	6
grapes	—	—	6	soon	short, temporary	—	18
habit	—	*mind* + *bound*	10	stayed	continued	—	17
hands	—	—	19	their	—	—	2
have	—	—	2	twelve	—	—	4
interest	—	—	1	ugly	grotesque	—	12
lady	—	*woman* + ruffles	13	uncle	—	*U* male	2
last	past, ago	—	20	week	—	—	20

Lesson 9

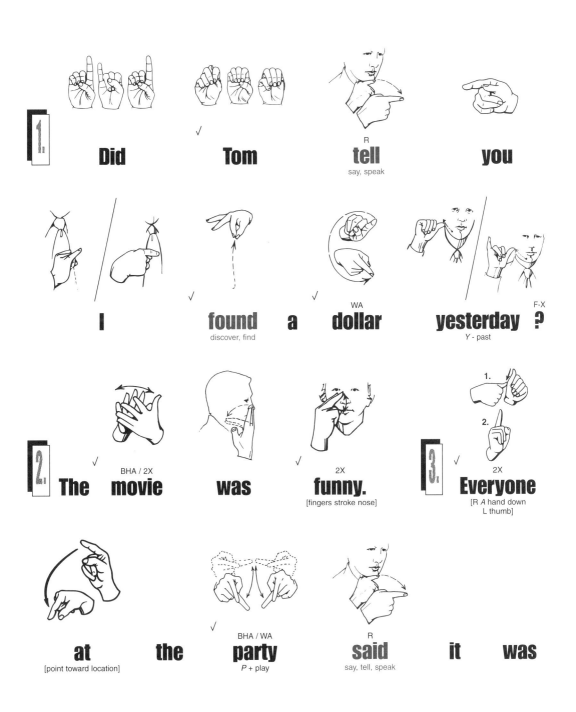

1. Did Tom tell [R] (say, speak) you I found [discover, find] a dollar [WA] yesterday [Y - past] ? [F-X]

2. The movie [BHA / 2X] was funny. [fingers stroke nose] [2X]

3. Everyone [R A hand down L thumb] [2X] at [point toward location] the party [BHA / WA] [P + play] said [R] (say, tell, speak) it was

fun.
BHA

Just
exactly

how much
a lot of, amount
[comparative or quantity]

do

you

want
L→B
long for, desire,
wish

for
WA

the

next

picture ?
F-X
[*C* hand]

5. **The**

car
BHA
drive

was

hidden
R-U-L
hide

behind
RHA

the

house.
BHA
building

6. **You**

must
EA / 2X
need, have to,
ought, should

go
BHA / AA   OUT / →R
went
opposite of *come*

with

him.

7. **Let**
WA
allow, may

them

leave
L→B
left, depart

if
BHA / AA
F hands

they   **desire.**
L→B
long for, want, wish

8.   **I**   **will**
shall, would

see   **you**   **tomorrow.**   **9.**   **Did**
saw

you   **look at**   **the**   **sunrise**   **or**
watch for

sunset   **yesterday ?**   **10.**   **I**
F-X
Y - past

hope   **you**   **will**   **watch for**   **him.**
expect, anticipate   shall, would   look for

11. **Did** **you** **arrive** **here** **by**
R-in-L

airplane ? **12.** **How many** **miles** **is it**
R→L F-X

to **Kansas City ?** **13.** **The** **children**
CW F-X F→R
KC child
[pat heads of children]

play **well** **together.** **14.** **I**
WA R-in-L C-C-W / BHA
[Y hands] with, circled

don't like **that** **man/** **woman!**
R R-in-L
[8 hand]

15. The   minute   I   left   the   room

L→B
leave, depart

[*R* hands]

he   began   talking.   **16.** The

R-in-L / WA
start, instituted,
initially

2X

BHA / AA

hours   seem like   days   when   you

R / WA

WA
appear,
look like

RHA

RHA   BHA

are   bored.   **17.** Who   will

dry under chin

C-C-W

shall, would

come   from   the   fields

BHA / AA   R→B
opposite of *go*

C-C-W

√ RHA / WA F-X
after a while ?
later

18. √ R-on-L
Next week **is** **the** **last**
skips a week final, end

of **the** 2X
√
month. **19.** **Are** **you**

F→R
planning **to** BHA / AA **come** R→B √ R-in-L **back** √ F-X **next year ?**
preparing, arranging opposite of go again year + 1→future
[P hands]

20. √
Last year **it** **was** **cold** **at** **this** √ RHA **time.**
a year ago winter now, (age, historical)
year + 1→past here [T hand]

Fingerspelling Practice Drills

("oo" words)

boon, raccoon, coon, food, noon, good, hood, look, too, took, mood, noodle, wool, pool, room, soon, stool, woolly, zoo, nook, book

81 82 83 84 85 86 87 88 89 90

Practice Sentences

1. Everyone left the room, when they came back.
2. We looked at the sunset from an airplane.
3. We visited her aunt, nephew, and cousin.
4. Next month we plan to grow flowers.
5. I hope it is warmer tomorrow than today.
6. Next year, let my husband go to the party.
7. Last year at this time it was cold in the fields.
8. Next week the children will all play together.
9. My brother is married.
10. Most of the children had dirty feet.
11. My pastor is from England.
12. The teacher told the students to review.
13. Families from Holland walk to church.
14. I went to the movie with John yesterday.
15. She was bored at the meeting Monday.
16. Watch for the children to come home.
17. It seems like winter, not spring.
18. My aunt met a gentleman in France.
19. My grandmother is visiting my cousin.
20. Next week we will see a movie.
21. Do you want a dollar?
22. The picture of the president is ugly.
23. The airplane left slowly.
24. Your face is really beautiful.

New Signs List

Word	Synonym	Memory Aid	Sentence	Word	Synonym	Memory Aid	Sentence
after a while	later	—	17	look at	watch for	—	9
airplane	—	—	11	man	—	—	14
back	again	—	19	many	—	—	12
behind	—	—	5	miles	—	—	12
bored	—	dry under chin	16	minute	—	—	15
by	—	—	11	month	—	—	18
car	drive	—	5	movie	—	—	2
dollar	—	—	1	next	—	—	4
don't like	—	—	14	next week	—	skips a week	18
everyone	—	—	3	next year	—	*year* + *1* →future	19
fields	—	—	17	party	—	*P* + play	3
found	discover, find	—	1	play	—	—	13
fun	—	—	3	room	—	—	15
funny	—	—	2	seem like	appear, look like	—	16
hidden	hide	—	5	sunrise	—	—	9
hope	expect, anticipate	—	10	sunset	—	—	9
hours	—	—	16	them	—	—	7
how much	a lot of, amount	—	4	time (age, historical)	—	—	20
if	—	—	7	Tom	—	—	1
just	exactly	—	4	watch for	look for	—	10
Kansas City	—	*K.C.*	12	well	—	—	13
last	final, end	—	18	who (question)	—	—	17
last year	a year ago	*year* + *1* →past	20	woman	—	—	14
let	allow, may	—	7	—	—	—	17

Lesson 10

1. ✓

A year ago
last year
year + 1 →past

today
now + day

the

weather

was

✓
C-C-W
beautiful.
pretty, lovely,
beauty

2. ✓
Two years from now
years + 2 + future

I

will
shall, would

be

✓
twenty

✓
years

old.
age
beard [*O* hand]

3.
Last
past, ago

✓
night
evening

I

saw
see

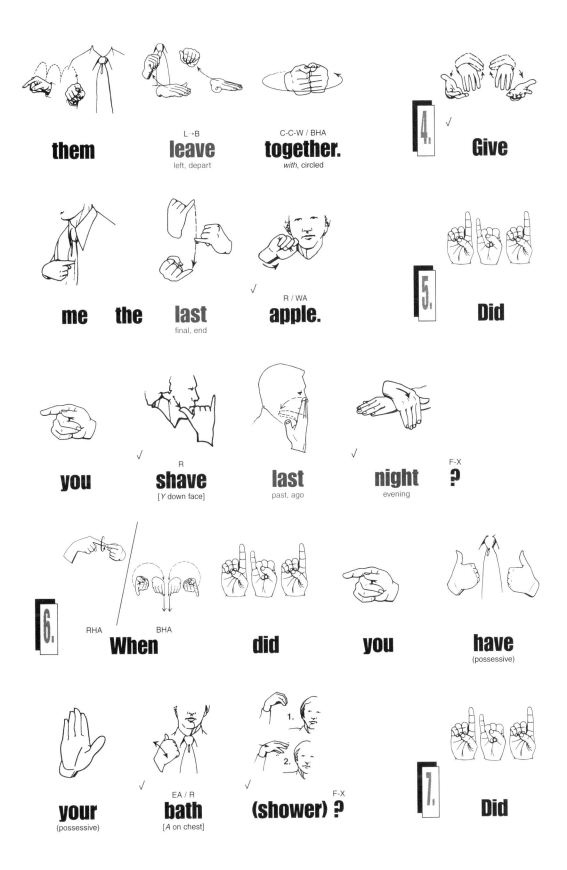

them

leave
L→B
left, depart

together.
C-C-W / BHA
with, circled

4. ✓ **Give**

me   **the**   **last**
final, end

apple.
R / WA
✓

5.   **Did**

you

shave
R
[*Y* down face]
✓

last
past, ago

night
evening
✓

?
F-X

6.   **When**
RHA   BHA

did

you

have
(possessive)

your
(possessive)

bath
EA / R
[*A* on chest]
✓

(shower) ?
F-X
✓

7.   **Did**

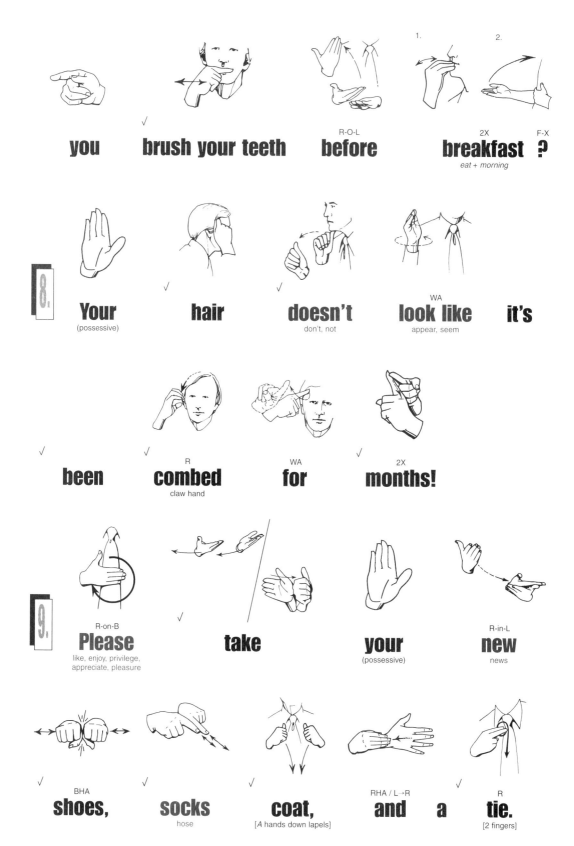

✓

you **brush your teeth** **before** **breakfast ?**

R-O-L

2X F-X

eat + morning

8. **Your** **hair** **doesn't** **look like** **it's**

(possessive) ✓ ✓ WA

don't, not appear, seem

✓ ✓ ✓

been **combed** **for** **months!**

R WA 2X

claw hand

9. **Please** **take** **your** **new**

R-on-B ✓ (possessive) R-in-L

like, enjoy, privilege, news
appreciate, pleasure

✓ ✓ ✓ RHA / L→R ✓

shoes, **socks** **coat,** **and** **a** **tie.**

BHA hose [A hands down lapels] R

[2 fingers]

10. **You** **are** **only** **a** **young** **man.**
C-C-W / EA · alone, someone · 2X · youthful

11. **Tell** **me** **the** **complete** **story.**
R · say, speak · all · 2X

12. **Can** **you** **fix** **the** **hem**
could, able, power · WA

of **my** **shirt ?** **13.** **The**
R-on-B · mine · [touch chest] · F-X · [pull twice]

room **was** **left** **empty.** **14.** **Was**
[R hands] · F→L · leave, abandon · R-on-L · naked, bare

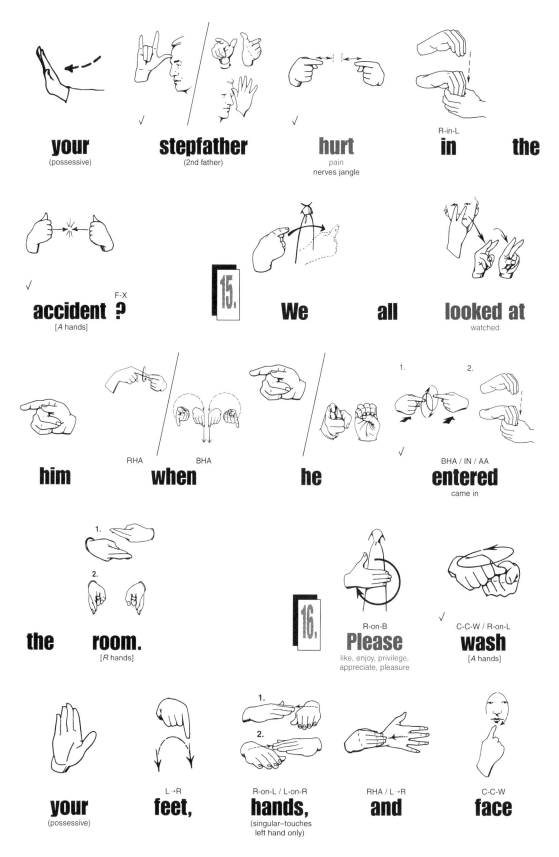

your
(possessive)

√ **stepfather**
(2nd father)

√ **hurt**
pain
nerves jangle

R-in-L
in

the

√ **accident** ? F-X
[*A* hands]

15.

We

all

looked at
watched

him

RHA   **when**   BHA

he

1.   2.
√
BHA / IN / AA
entered
came in

1.   2.
the   **room.**
[*R* hands]

16.

R-on-B
Please
like, enjoy, privilege,
appreciate, pleasure

√ C-C-W / R-on-L
wash
[*A* hands]

your
(possessive)

L→R
feet,

1.   2.
R-on-L / L-on-R
hands,
(singular–touches
left hand only)

RHA / L→R
and

C-C-W
face

before
R-O-L

going
BHA / AA   OUT / →R
went
opposite of *come*

to

bed.
✓

17.
You

should
EA / 2X
need, have to,
ought, must

be

kind
✓
(emotion)

to

old
age
beard [*O* hand]

people.
BHA / IN / EA / AA
[*P* hands]

18.

Some
R-in-L
part

children
F→R
child
[pat heads of children]

are
✓

mean
cruel

to

animals.
BHA / 2X

19.

Do

you

understand
RHA
recognize
light goes on

what

I

mean
R-in-L / WA   F-X
intend, purpose

?
1.
2.
✓

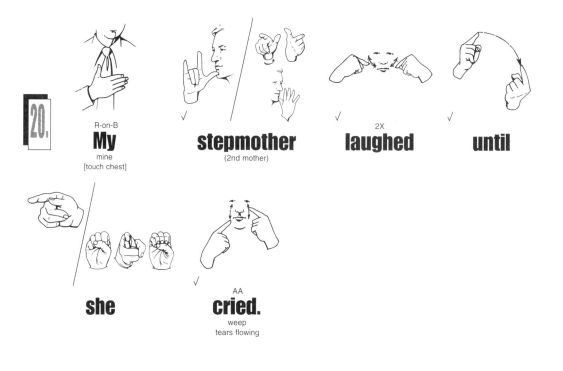

20.

My
R-on-B
mine
[touch chest]

stepmother ✓
(2nd mother)

laughed ✓
2X

until ✓

she

cried. ✓
AA
weep
tears flowing

Fingerspelling Practice Drills
("ei" words)

being, feint, deign, receive, either, conceive, heist, ceiling, neither, weird

91 92 93 94 95 96 97 98 99 100

Practice Sentences

1. My stepmother washed her hands.
2. Please comb your hair and wash your face.
3. Twenty years ago the weather was beautiful.
4. Will you comb your hair and shave please?
5. I cried when my uncle was in the accident.
6. Apples are good for young men.
7. Can you tell me about the empty room?
8. Please take some coffee to drink.
9. Yesterday we were in an accident.
10. My brother is mean to us.
11. The weather was beautiful last night.
12. The young man told me a story.
13. Did you have a bath or a shower last night?
14. He was in pain for months after the accident.
15. After the accident the stepfather fixed the car.
16. Some children are cruel to old people.
17. Old people are kind to children and animals.
18. The minute he left, the party was boring.
19. Her sister found three turtles in the field.
20. Animals are mean when hurt.
21. After breakfast I brushed my teeth.
22. A year ago the president went to Italy.
23. Please tell me the complete story.
24. He left his coat and tie in the room.

New Signs List

Word	Synonym	Memory Aid	Sentence	Word	Synonym	Memory Aid	Sentence
accident	—	—	14	mean	cruel	—	18
apple	—	—	4	mean	intend, purpose	—	19
bath	—	—	6	night	evening	—	3,5
bed	—	—	16	shave	—	—	5
brush your teeth	—	—	7	shirt	—	—	12
coat	—	—	9	shoes	—	—	9
combed	—	claw hand	8	shower	—	—	6
complete	all	—	11	socks	hose	—	9
cried	weep	tears flowing	20	stepfather	—	—	14
doesn't	don't, not	—	8	stepmother	—	—	20
empty	naked, bare	—	13	take	—	—	9
entered	—	came in	15	tie	—	—	9
fix	—	—	12	twenty	—	—	2
give	—	—	4	two years from now	—	*years + 2 + future*	2 9
hair	—	—	8	until	—	—	20
hem	—	—	12	wash	—	—	16
hurt	pain	nerves jangle	14	weather	—	—	1
kind (emotion)	—	—	17	young	youthful	—	10
laugh	—	—	20	years (future)	—	—	2

Lesson 11

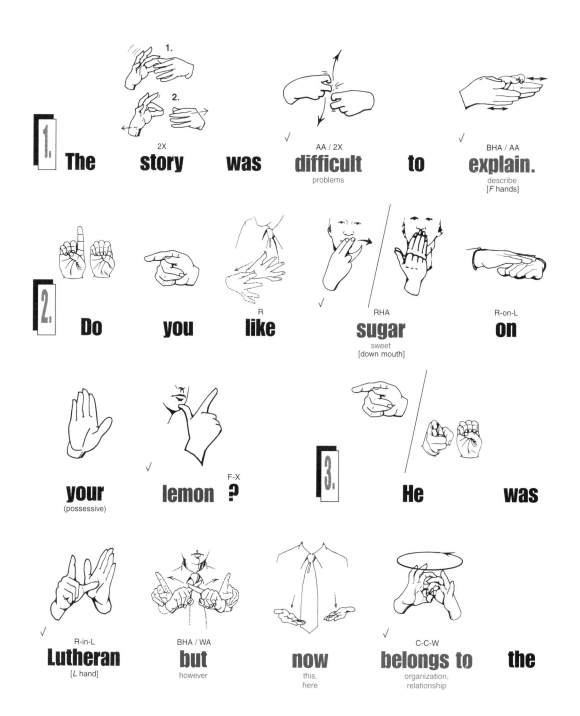

1. The   story   was   √ **difficult**   to   √ **explain.**

2X   AA / 2X   BHA / AA
problems   describe [*F* hands]

2. Do   you   like   √ **sugar**   on

R   RHA   R-on-L
sweet [down mouth]

your   √ **lemon** **?**   **3.** He   was

(possessive)   F-X

Lutheran   **but**   **now**   √ **belongs to**   the

√ R-in-L   BHA / WA   C-C-W
[*L* hand]   however   this, here   organization, relationship

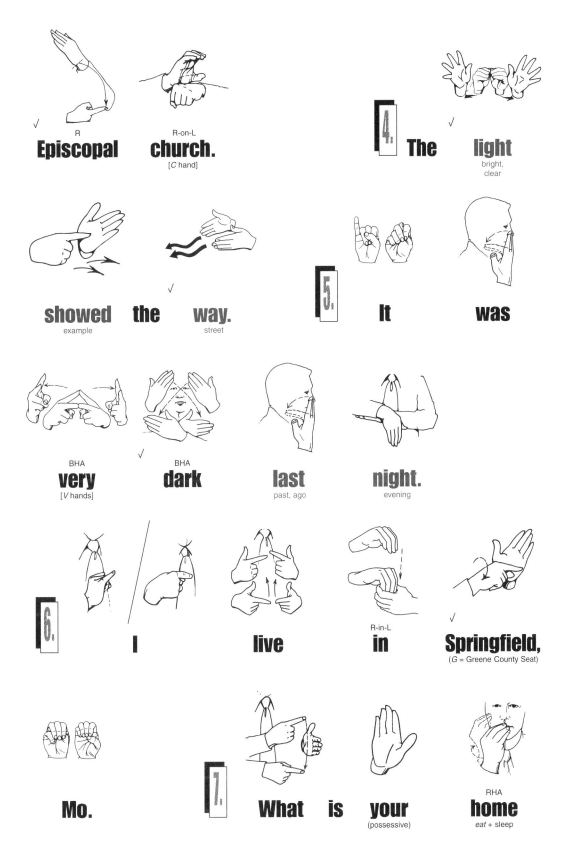

Episcopal
R

church.
R-on-L
[*C* hand]

4. **The**

light
bright,
clear

showed
example

the

way.
street

5. **It**

was

very
BHA
[*V* hands]

dark
BHA

last
past, ago

night.
evening

6. **I**

live

in
R-in-L

Springfield,
(*G* = Greene County Seat)

Mo.

7. **What**

is

your
(possessive)

home
RHA
eat + sleep

address ?
F-X
A like *live*

8.

How
BHA

long
continue, stay

have

you

lived

there ?
R   F-X

9.

Time
R-on-L
wristwatch

is short.
R-on-L
soon,
temporary

10.

Maybe
AA
possibly,
perhaps, might

you

should
EA / 2X
need, have to,
ought, must

come
BHA / AA   R→B
opposite of *go*

back
R-in-L
again

tomorrow.

11.

The

man

struck
hit, strike

the

rock
R-on-L

only
alone, someone
C-C-W / EA

√

once.
R-in-L

12. √ **Sometimes**
once in a while,
occasionally
R-in-L / 2X

we

go
went
opposite of *come*
BHA / AA

to
OUT / →R

a

√ **restaurant**
(*R* at mouth)
R

after
across
RL

church.
[*C* hand]
R-on-L

13. **May**
let,
allow

I

√ **use**
[*U* circled]
CW

your
(possessive)

car
drive
BHA

√ **tonight** **?**
now + night
F-X

14. **Please**
like, enjoy, privilege,
appreciate, pleasure
R-on-B

√ **open** **the** √ **window.**
R-on-L

15. √ **Close** **the**
opposite of
open

door

R-on-B
please.
like, enjoy, privilege,
appreciate, pleasure

16. The

R→L
airplane

flew

R-O-L
over
above

R-on-B
my
mine
[touch chest]

BHA
house
building

recently.
[finger action]

17.

F→R
Put
place

your
(possessive)

R-on-L / L-on-R
hands
(singular–right hand
touches left only)

R-on-L
on

the

table.
rest arm on table / 4 legs and a top

18.

Will
shall, would

you

→L
run

2X / R-U-L
a

OUT / AA
race
compete,
competition, contest

with

me

F-X
?

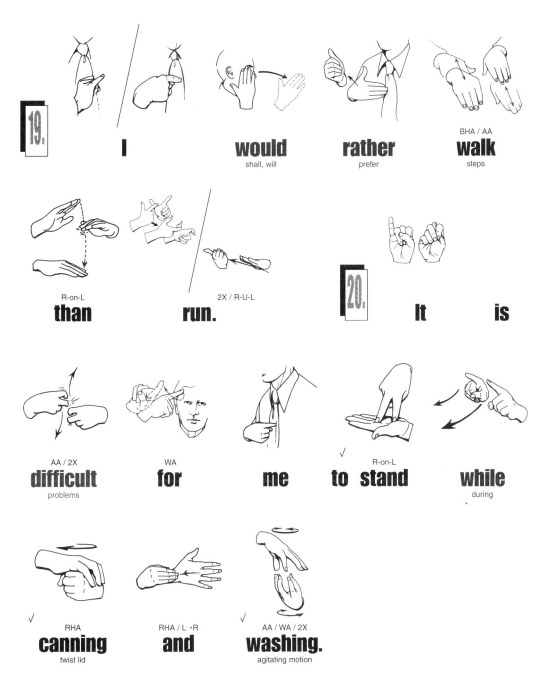

19.

I

would
shall, will

rather
prefer

BHA / AA
walk
steps

R-on-L
than

2X / R-U-L
run.

20.

It

is

AA / 2X
difficult
problems

WA
for

me

√
R-on-L
to stand

while
during

√
RHA
canning
twist lid

RHA / L→R
and

√
AA / WA / 2X
washing.
agitating motion

Fingerspelling Practice Drills
("ie" words)

bier, died, fiery, lied, client, piece, pierce, tier, vizier, believe

101 102 103 104 105 106 107 108 109 110

Practice Sentences

1. He struck the rock.
2. I told the story about the airplane race.
3. She washed the window recently.
4. Wash your hands before you go to the table.
5. It is difficult to explain how dark it was.
6. The window on the plane was open.
7. I ran only once to the table in the house.
8. The man visited the Catholic church.
9. Maybe we should meet at the restaurant.
10. May we drink lemonade after we return?
11. I like sugar in my tea.
12. They went to a restaurant after the race.
13. Once in a while he will call on me in class.
14. My mother put sugar in the lemonade.
15. The story told in the dark was short.
16. The restaurant used lemon in the tea.
17. Sometimes she drinks lemonade.
18. Do you go to the Episcopal church?
19. He would like sugar in his coffee.
20. She struck the door once and it closed.
21. I go to church near the restaurant.
22. I will start running early in the day.
23. She recently drove her mother's car.
24. Mother saw a light in the house.

New Signs List

Word	Synonym	Memory Aid	Sentence	Word	Synonym	Memory Aid	Sentence
address	—	A like *live*	7	over	above	—	16
belongs to	organization, relationship	—	3	race	compete, competition, contest	—	18
canning	—	twist lid	20	recently	—	—	16
close (shut)	—	opposite of *open*	15	restaurant	—	—	12
dark	—	—	5	rock	—	—	11
difficult	problems	—	1,20	sometimes	once in a while, occasionally	—	12
door	—	—	15	Springfield	—	—	6
Episcopal	—	—	3	stand	—	—	20
explain	describe	—	1	struck	hit, strike	—	11
flew	—	—	16	sugar	sweet	—	2
lemon	—	—	2	there	—	—	8
light	bright, clear	—	4	tonight	—	*now + night*	13
Lutheran	—	—	3	use	—	—	13
maybe	possibly, perhaps, might	—	10	washing	—	agitating motion	20
once	—	—	11	way	street	—	4
open	—	—	14	window	—	—	14

Lesson 12

1.

Would
shall, will

you

please
R-on-B
like, enjoy, privilege,
appreciate, pleasure

sit down/
sat, chair

be seated.

2.

Be careful
watch out
2X

or

you

will
shall, would

fall.
[stand, then fall]

3.

You

say
R
tell, speak

you

are

right,
R-on-L
just, correct

but
BHA / WA
however

I

think
thought

you

are

wrong.
mistake, error
[Y below chin]

4.

They | won't | play | fairly.
refuse | R | WA | R-in-L
| | [Y hands] | even, equal

5.

We | thought | we | would | win
| think | | shall, will | BHA / RHA
| | | | get + wave flag

that | game, | but | we | lost.
R-in-L | challenge | BHA / WA | | R-in-L
| | however | | [V hands]

6.

The | flag | is | sometimes | called | "the
| RHA | | R-in-L / 2X | BHA |
| | | once in a while, occasionally | named |

red, | white, | and | blue."
R | R | RHA / L→R | R / WA
lips | shirt | | [B hand]
| [open 5 hand] | |

7.

John

had
(possessive)

a

✓ R / WA
yellow

shirt,
[pull twice]

✓ R / WA
a

blue
[*B* hand]

coat,
[*A* hands down lapels]

RHA / L→R
and

a

✓ R / WA
green
[*G* hand]

R
tie.
[2 fingers]

8.

R-in-L
Some
part

R-in-L / 2X
spring
grow

R→L
flowers
smell

✓ R / WA
are

purple.
[*P* hand]

9.

RHA
Most

✓ WA
trees
[5 hand]

have
(possessive)

✓ **black**
eyebrows

✓ **bark.**

10.

Do

you

like

R
pink
[P on lips]

lemonade

F-X
?

11. They

R-on-L
painted
[paint back and forth]

their

BHA
house
building

R
white
shirt
[open 5 hand]

with

R
brown
[B down R cheek]

trim.

12. The

L→R / BHA / C-C-W
clouds

are

a

gray

WF
color

today.
now + day

13. He

R
said,
say, tell, speak

"It

is

RHA
not fair
[F hands]

R-in-L
to ride
(in a car)

with

me."

14.
Would
shall, will

you

R
like

√ R-on-L
to ride

√
a

R
horse

F-X
?

15. √ WA / BHA
Turn

√ R→L
left

at

the

next

corner.

16.
He

lives

R-in-L
in

√
the

RHA / WA
third

BHA
house
building

R-on-L
on

the

√ R
right.
[R →right direction]

17.
Do

you

prefer
rather

music F-X **?**
M + song

18. **Yes,** 2X / WA

I

like R

Spanish BHA
Spain

music. M + song

19. **It** **is** **time** R-on-L
wristwatch

to start R-in-L / WA
begin,
instituted, initially

working R-on-L / 2X
labor,
job

hard.

20. **Do** **you** **have**
(possessive)

the **keys** WA **to park**

my R-on-B
mine
[touch chest]

car BHA F-X **?**
drive

Fingerspelling Practice Drills

("oe" words)

aloes, coerce, foe, doer, doe, hoe, Joe, poem, shoes, toes, poet, roe, woes

111 112 113 114 115 116 117 118 119 120

Practice Sentences

1. The music was difficult in Spanish.
2. The lady started to paint her house.
3. I left my keys in the car next to your house.
4. I prefer to eat green grapes and brown gravy.
5. The Spanish boy had a brown horse.
6. It was wrong to start the car.
7. Sometimes we call James twice a week.
8. I painted the car black.
9. We had pink lemonade after the game.
10. They lost the game.
11. The game was not fair.
12. The horse lost the race.
13. The flowers were yellow, purple, and green.
14. I live in the house on the right.
15. Did we win or lose?
16. Be careful riding the horse, so you won't fall.
17. Paul thinks you are always wrong.
18. The preacher found his book while riding.
19. They lost the football game last night.
20. The house was green with purple and red.
21. My car key is yellow.
22. His face is black and blue.
23. I didn't teach the horse to go left.
24. I think you are wrong; the house was red.

New Signs List

Word	Synonym	Memory Aid	Sentence	Word	Synonym	Memory Aid	Sentence
bark	—	—	9	painted	—	—	11
be careful	watch out	—	2	park	—	—	20
be seated	—	—	1	pink	—	—	10
black	—	eyebrow	9	purple	—	—	8
blue	—	—	6,7	red	—	lips	6
brown	—	—	11	ride (car)	—	—	13
clouds	—	—	12	ride (horse)	—	—	14
color	—	—	12	right (direction)	—	—	16
fairly	even, equal	—	4	right	just, correct	—	3
fall	—	—	2	sit down	chair, sat	—	1
flag	—	—	6	Spanish	Spain	—	18
game	challenge	—	5	third	—	—	16
gray	—	—	12	trees	—	—	9
green	—	—	7	trim	—	—	11
hard	—	—	19	turn	—	—	15
horse	—	—	14	white	—	shirt	6,11
keys	—	—	20	win	—	get + wave flag	5
left (direction)	—	—	15	won't	refuse	—	4
lemonade	—	—	10	wrong	mistake, error	—	3
lost (game)	—	—	5	yellow	—	—	7
music	—	M + song	17,18	yes	—	—	18
not fair	—	—	13	" "	—	—	6

Lesson 13

R-in-L
Stop **at** **the** **store** **and** **buy**
sell,
sales, shops
purchase
money paid out

  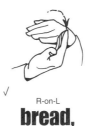 

R-in-L R-on-L R / WA
me **some** **bread,** **fish,** **melons,**

RHA / L→R
and **bananas.** **It** **is**

  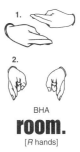

R-in-L BHA
warm **in** **this** **room.**
[blowing on hand] now,
here
[R hands]

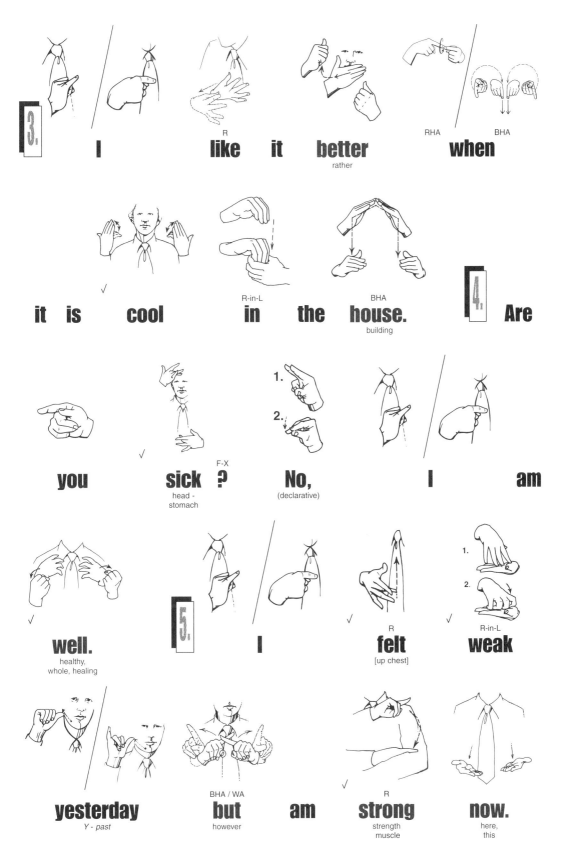

I   **like**   **it**   **better**   **when**

R   rather   RHA   BHA

it   **is**   **cool**   **in**   **the**   **house.**   **Are**

R-in-L   BHA — building

you   **sick ?**   **No,**   **I**   **am**

head - stomach   F-X   (declarative)

well.   **I**   **felt**   **weak**

healthy, whole, healing   R [up chest]   R-in-L

yesterday   **but**   **am**   **strong**   **now.**

Y - past   BHA / WA — however   R — strength muscle   here, this

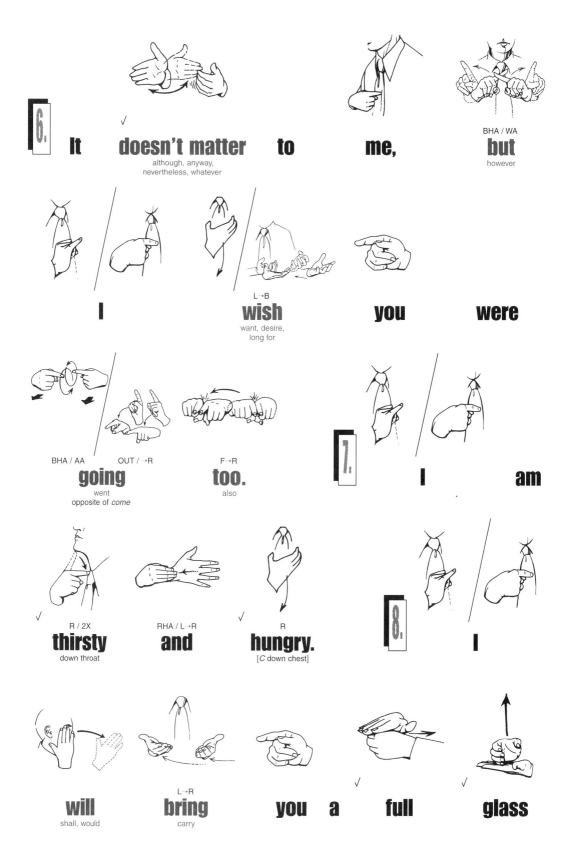

6. ✓

It   doesn't matter   to   me,   but

although, anyway,
nevertheless, whatever

BHA / WA
however

I   wish   you   were

L→B
want, desire,
long for

going   too.   7.   I   am

BHA / AA   OUT / →R

went
opposite of *come*

F→R
also

✓
thirsty   and   hungry.   8.   I

R / 2X
down throat

RHA / L→R

✓
R
[*C* down chest]

will   bring   you   a   full   glass

shall, would

L→R
carry

✓   ✓

of　**water.**
[*W* at mouth]
2X

9.　**When**
RHA　　　BHA

I

visited　**their**　**home,**　**I**　**saw**
[*V* hands]　　　　　RHA　　　　　　see
　　　　　　　　　eat + sleep

rats　**and**　**mice.**　**10.**　**The**
[*R* hand, brush nose]　RHA / L→R　[forefinger like *rats*,
R / 2X　　　　　　　　R / 2X　brush nose]

rooster　**awakened**　**us**　**early**　**in**
[*3* at forehead]　eyes open　　　　R-on-L　　R-in-L

the　**morning.**　**11.**　**I**　**heard**
R　　　　　　　　　　　　　　　listen
sun comes up　　　　　　　　　　[*C* at R ear]

the   owl   screaming   all night.   **12.**   He

shout
[C up]

RHA

read   us   stories   from   Greece

eyes scanning book

1.

2.

2X

[G at bridge of nose]

and   Rome.   **13.**   The   person

RHA / L→R

[R at bridge of nose]

personal
[P hands]

who   comes   from   Africa

C-C-W

BHA / AA   R→B

opposite of go

RHA / C-C-W

[A hand]

appreciates   America.   **14.**   How   did

R-on-B

like, enjoy,
pleases, pleasure

C-C-W

rail fence

BHA

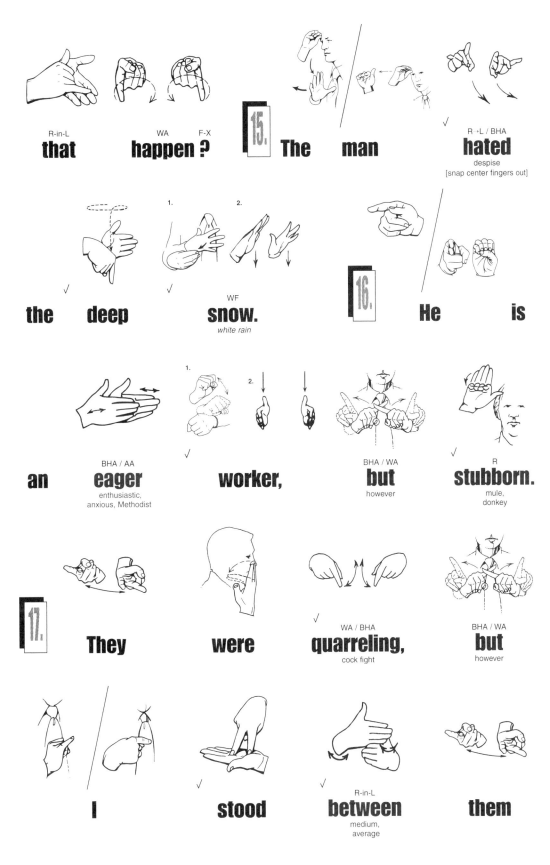

R-in-L **that**	WA **happen** F-X **?**	**15.** **The**	**man**	√ R→L / BHA **hated** despise [snap center fingers out]	

the **deep** 1. 2. WF **snow.** white rain

16. **He** **is**

an BHA / AA **eager** enthusiastic, anxious, Methodist | 1. 2. √ **worker,** | BHA / WA **but** however | √ R **stubborn.** mule, donkey

17. **They** **were** √ WA / BHA **quarreling,** cock fight | BHA / WA **but** however

I √ **stood** √ R-in-L **between** medium, average | **them**

RHA / L→R
and

R-in-L
stopped

them.

18.
Don't
not

✓
R-in-L
bother
disturb

me

RHA   BHA
when

I

2X   BHA / AA
am   **talking!**

19.
You

CW
always
ever

✓
R-in-L
interrupt

me!

20.
Will
shall, would

you

✓
R-on-L / 2X
print
newspaper
Linotype

this

1.
2.
✓
program
[*P* hand]

WA
for

me   F-X
?

Fingerspelling Practice Drills

("qu" words)

quad, quiz, quick, quack, equal, quill, equate, squawk, square, quorum, sequel, quarry, squall, mosque, squalid, acquire, quarter, quantity, quizzical, quake

121 122 123 124 125 126 127 128 129 130

Practice Sentences

1. The bread was still warm when I bought it.
2. I am thirsty; please bring me a drink of water.
3. Don't interrupt me when I am talking.
4. The stories he read were about an owl.
5. When I visited Rome, I quarreled with a man.
6. If you eat fish with bananas, you will be sick.
7. You need to buy a cat to eat our rats.
8. Stop quarreling and print the story.
9. My brother was awakened by a scream.
10. The owl was really screaming.
11. The whiskey was expensive.
12. I doubt if the bananas smell very good.
13. We had eggs in our kitchen.
14. She likes fish with her bread.
15. It is warm here, but I like it cool.
16. He is feeling weak today.
17. I am so hungry I could eat a rat.
18. Have you printed the program yet?
19. When I am thirsty I drink water.
20. When it was snowing we saw mice.
21. The program was shown in the morning.
22. She hated to be interrupted.
23. Quarreling made them weak and sick.
24. The roosters awakened them early.

New Signs List

Word	Synonym	Memory Aid	Sentence	Word	Synonym	Memory Aid	Sentence
Africa	—	—	13	morning	—	sun comes up	10
all night	—	—	11	owl	—	—	11
America	—	rail fence	13	print	newspaper	Linotype	20
awakened	—	eyes open	10	program	—	—	20
bananas	—	—	1	quarreling	—	cock fights	17
between	medium, average	—	17	rats	—	—	9
bother	disturb	—	18	Rome	—	—	12
bread	—	—	1	rooster	—	—	10
cool	—	—	3	screaming	shouting	—	11
deep	—	—	15	sick	—	head, stomach	4
doesn't matter	although, anyway, nevertheless, whatever	—	6	snow	—	*white rain*	15
felt	—	—	5	stood	—	—	17
fish	—	—	1	stop	—	—	1,17
full	—	—	8	store	sell, sales, shops	—	1
glass	—	—	8	strong	strength	muscle	5
Greece	—	—	12	stubborn	mule, donkey	—	16
hated	despised	—	15	thirsty	—	down throat	7
heard	listen	—	11	warm	—	—	2
hungry	—	—	7	water	—	—	8
interrupt	—	—	19	weak	—	—	5
melons	—	—	1	well	healthy, whole, healing	—	4
mice	—	—	9	worker	—	—	16

Lesson 14

1. **Many** **hearing**
2X
speaking

people **are** **ignorant**
BHA / IN / EA / AA
[P hands]
√
R
[V on forehead]

about **the** **deaf.**
CW

2. **The** **reason** **for**
C-C-W
cause, excuse
[R]
WA

this **is** **they** **misunderstand** **each other.**
now,
here
√
R / WA
twisted in the mind
[mean, intend on forehead]
√
R-O-L / BHA
fellowship, stir (emotion),
one another

3. **We** **must** **be careful** **not** **to complain**
EA / 2X
need, have to,
ought, should
2X
watch out
[V hands, sign keep twice]
don't
√
2X
gripe, grumble,
object (verb) 1X

CW
about

them.

4.

Would
shall, will

you

R-on-B
please
like, enjoy, privilege,
appreciate, pleasure

R-in-L
bake
cook

me

R-in-L
some
part

WA / R-in-L
cookies,
[cutting out cookies]

a

R-in-L
cake,
hot cross buns

RHA / L→R
and

a

R-in-L   F-X
pie   ?
slicing pie wedge

5.

I

OUT
ordered

R-in-L
some
part

R-on-L
bread,

R-in-L
butter,

2X
jelly,

RHA / L→R
and

doughnuts.
[*R* hands at mouth]

6.

Do

you

R-on-B
like
please, enjoy, privilege,
appreciate, pleasure

√   2X

a   **little**

√   BHA / AA / 2X

milk

R-in-L

in

√

your
(possessive)

√

cup

of

R-in-L / WA   F-X

tea   **?**

7.

I

R

like

√

vinegar
[*V* at mouth]

R-on-L

on

R-on-B

my
mine
[touch chest]

salad

with

√   2X

salt

RHA / L →R

and

√   WA

pepper.

8.

He

√   R / 2X

smelled

strongly   **of**   √   **whiskey**

√

(vodka).
[*V* on back of hand]

9.

Can
could, able,
power

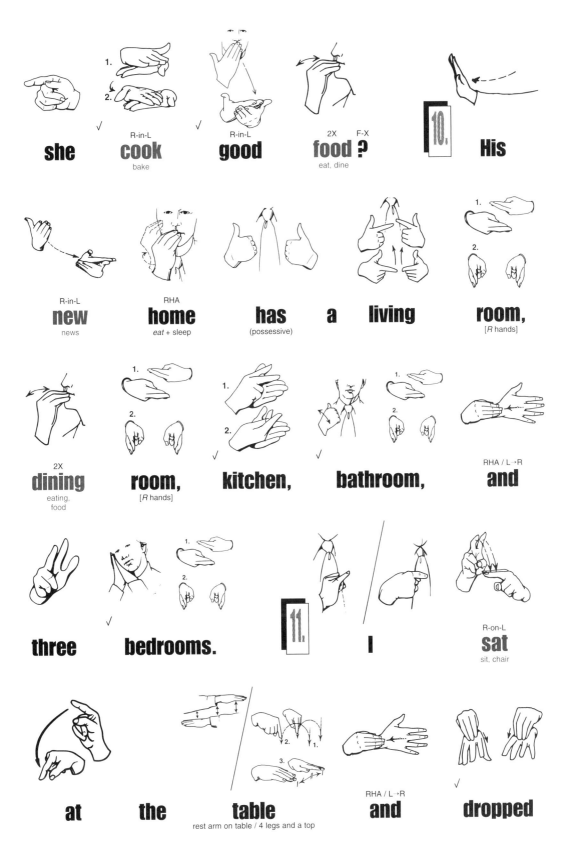

she | **cook** | **good** | **food ?** | **His**

R-in-L (bake) | R-in-L | 2X F-X (eat, dine) | 10.

new | **home** | **has** | **a** | **living** | **room,**

R-in-L (news) | RHA (eat + sleep) | (possessive) | | | [*R* hands]

dining | **room,** | **kitchen,** | **bathroom,** | **and**

2X (eating, food) | [*R* hands] | | | RHA / L→R

three | **bedrooms.** | **I** | **sat**

11. | | | R-on-L (sit, chair)

at | **the** | **table** | **and** | **dropped**

rest arm on table / 4 legs and a top | RHA / L→R

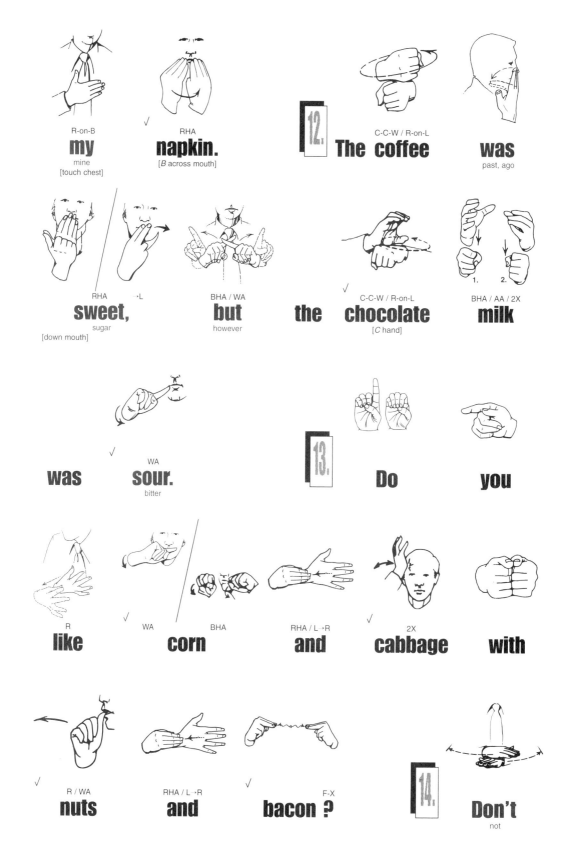

R-on-B
my
mine
[touch chest]

√
RHA
napkin.
[*B* across mouth]

12. **The coffee**

C-C-W / R-on-L
was
past, ago

RHA ·L
sweet,
sugar
[down mouth]

BHA / WA
but
however

the

√
C-C-W / R-on-L
chocolate
[*C* hand]

BHA / AA / 2X
milk
1. 2.

was

√
WA
sour.
bitter

13.

Do

you

R
like

√
WA
corn

BHA

RHA / L·R
and

√
2X
cabbage

with

√
R / WA
nuts

RHA / L·R
and

√
F-X
bacon ?

14.

Don't
not

bother
R-in-L
disturb

me,

I

am

too

busy.
business

15.

He

is

idle
WF
vacation

most
RHA

of

the

time;
R-on-L
wristwatch

I

say
R
tell,
speak

he

is

lazy.
R
[*L* on L shoulder]

16.

I

doubt
BHA / AA

if

he

really
[*R* like *true*]

has
(possessive)

F→R / BHA
as

much
a lot of, amount
[comparative or quantity]

R-in-L / 2X
money

F→R / BHA
as

he

R
says.
tells, speaks

17. ✓ **The**

R-on-L
ring
[*R* hand]

✓ WA
looks
appears, seems

✓ RHA
cheap,

BHA / WA
but
however

he

R
said
tell, speak

it

was

✓ R-in-L
expensive.

18. **One**

RHA
day

it

is

✓ RHA
1. 2.
dry

here,

RHA / L→R
and

the

1. 2.
next

day **it** **is** **wet.**
RHA
2X
soft, tender,
gentle

We
19.

had **a** **true** **and** **false** **test.**
(possessive)
R
sure
[up and out from mouth]
R
artificial, counterfeit
speak from side of mouth
BHA
questions, many

He **is** **a** **liar** **about**
20.
lie + person
CW

the **candy** **and** **gum.**
WA
sweet tooth
RHA / L→R
2X
Akron, OH;
rubber

Fingerspelling Practice Drills

("om" words)

bomb, comb, home, boom, romp, some, tome, Nome, axiom, momma, mommy, vomit, woman, foment, pompom, domestic

131 132 133 134 135 136 137 138 139 140

Practice Sentences

1. I made cake and pie for dinner.
2. The living room was painted blue.
3. We should be careful not to tell lies.
4. I ate nuts for lunch.
5. The milk was sour.
6. I like German chocolate cake.
7. It is sad when people misunderstand others.
8. The butter became sour in the warm room.
9. Please put butter and salt on the corn.
10. I like milk with my doughnuts.
11. That is an expensive ring.
12. I doubt that she will bake a cake.
13. He is ignorant about many things.
14. Please be careful!
15. She is a very good cook.
16. Would you like coffee and doughnuts?
17. They eat cookies and milk in the kitchen.
18. My teacher had some coffee and bread.
19. Paul has a rat in his kitchen.
20. My mother is a good cook.
21. Did you think he smelled of vodka?
22. The lazy man drinks cheap whiskey.
23. Please buy me some bacon and chocolate.
24. The pie in the kitchen had nuts in it.

New Signs List

Word	Synonym	Memory Aid	Sentence	Word	Synonym	Memory Aid	Sentence
bacon	—	—	13	jelly	—	—	5
bake	cook	—	4	kitchen	—	—	10
bathroom	—	—	10	lazy	—	—	15
bedroom	—	—	10	liar	—	lie + person	20
busy	business	—	14	little	—	—	6
butter	—	—	5	looks	appears, seems	—	17
cabbage	—	—	13	milk	—	—	6,12
cake	—	hot cross buns	4	misunderstand	—	twisted in the mind	2
candy	—	sweet tooth	20	napkin	—	—	11
cheap	—	—	17	nuts	—	—	13
chocolate	—	—	12	ordered (food)	—	—	5
complain	gripe, grumble, object 1x (v)	—	3	pepper	—	—	7
cook	—	—	9	pie	—	slicing pie wedge	4
cookies	—	—	4	really	—	—	16
corn	—	—	13	reason	cause, excuse	—	2
cup	—	—	6	ring	—	—	17
doubt	—	—	16	salt	—	—	7
doughnuts	—	—	5	smelled	—	—	8
drop	—	—	11	sour	bitter	—	12
dry	—	—	18	test	—	questions, many	19
each other	fellowship, stir, one another	—	2	too	—	—	14
expensive	—	—	17	vinegar	—	—	7
false	artificial, counterfeit	speak from side of mouth	19	vodka	—	—	8
gum	Akron, Ohio; rubber	—	20	wet	soft, tender, gentle	—	18
ignorant	—	—	1	whiskey	—	—	8

Lesson 15

1.

His   **friend**   **is**   **very**   **intelligent**   **(smart).**

hooked forefingers

BHA
[*V* hands]

[center finger from forehead]

[forefinger]

2.

What   **time**   **did**   **you**   **arrive ?**

R-on-L
wristwatch

F-X

3.

I   **am**   **planning**   **to**   **visit**

[*P* hands]   F→R
preparing, arranging

OUT / BHA / AA
[*V* hands]

my   **mother**   **and**   **father.**

R-on-B
mine
[touch chest]

RHA / L→R

4. **I**

R-on-B
enjoy
like, please, privilege,
appreciate, pleasure

R / OUT
traveling
trip, journey

with

R-on-B
my
mine
[touch chest]

R-U-L
assistant
[R hand lifts L]

BHA / AA
manager.
master

5. **I**

would
shall, will

rather
prefer

R-in-L
ride

a

R→L
plane

R-on-L
than

the

R-on-L
train
tracks

or

bus.

6. **I**

almost
barely

missed
absent

the

WF
fire.
flames

7. **The multiplication**
2X
worse **1X,**
multiply

test
BHA
questions,
many

was

✓

easy.
2X
simple

8.

He

has
(possessive)

a lot of
much, amount
[comparative or quantity]

✓

responsibility.
[2 *R's* on R shoulder]

9.
✓

To obey   **is**

better
rather

than
R-on-L

to disobey.
✓

10.

I

have
(possessive)

a

great
large, big

✓

burden
[open hands, like
responsibility]

to carry.
L→R

11.

I

visited
OUT / BHA / AA
[*V* hands]

a

✓

farm
L→R
beard
[5 hand under chin]

and
RHA / L→R

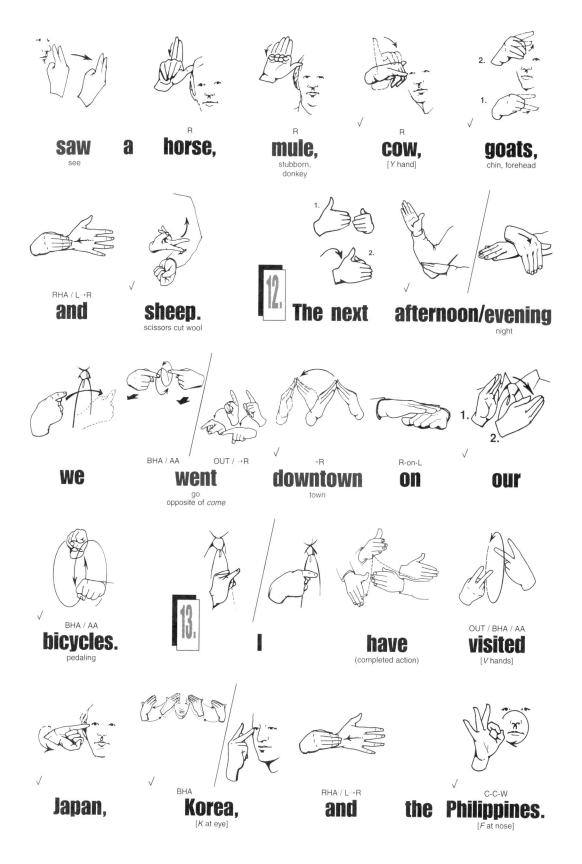

saw **a** **horse,** R

see

mule, R

stubborn, donkey

cow, R

[Y hand]

goats, R

chin, forehead

and

RHA / L→R

sheep.

scissors cut wool

12. **The next**

afternoon/evening

night

we

went

BHA / AA   OUT / →R

go

opposite of *come*

downtown

→R

town

on

R-on-L

our

bicycles.

BHA / AA

pedaling

13. **I**

have

(completed action)

visited

OUT / BHA / AA

[V hands]

Japan,

Korea,

BHA

[K at eye]

and

RHA / L→R

the **Philippines.**

C-C-W

[F at nose]

14.

I

would
shall, will

R
like

you

to stay
continue

with

me

F→R / BHA
as

R-in-L / 2X
often
again & again

F→R / BHA
as

you

can.
could, able,
power

15.

We

✓
agree
think - same

CW
about

so

2.

1.
many

✓
F→R
things,

BHA / WA
but
however

I

✓
disagree
think - opposite

with

you

CW
about

this.
now,
here

16.

If
BHA / AA
[*F* hands,
thumbs strike]

you

continue
stay, still

to quarrel
WA / BHA
cock fight

with

me,

I

will
shall, would

become

angry.
wrath, anger
[sign at waist]

17.

I

notice

you

are

very
BHA
[*V* hands]

calm
quiet, still

about
CW

it.

18.

I

understand
RHA
recognize
light goes on

you

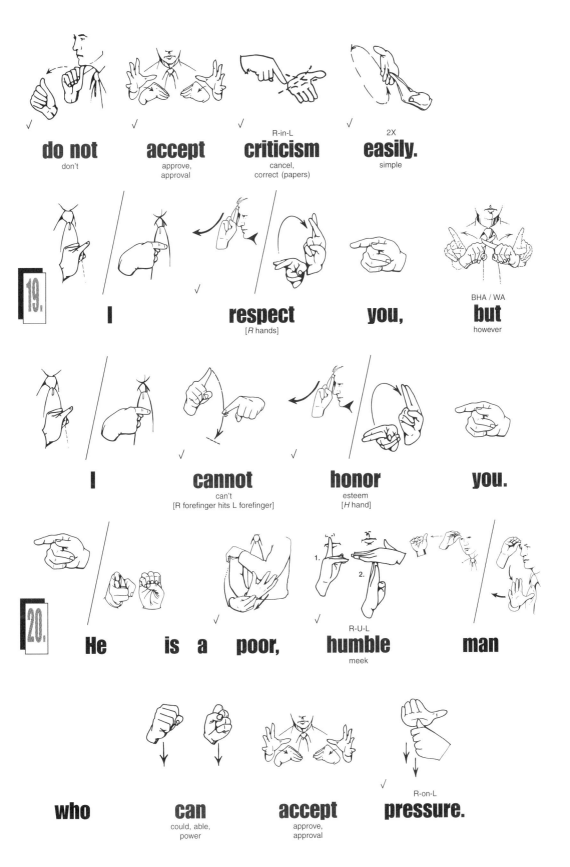

do not
don't

accept
approve,
approval

R-in-L
criticism
cancel,
correct (papers)

2X
easily.
simple

19.

I

respect
[*R* hands]

you,

BHA / WA
but
however

I

cannot
can't
[R forefinger hits L forefinger]

honor
esteem
[*H* hand]

you.

20.

He   **is**   **a**   **poor,**

R-U-L
humble
meek

man

who

can
could, able,
power

accept
approve,
approval

R-on-L
pressure.

Fingerspelling Practice Drills

("on" words)

aeons, bone, cone, done, eons, neon, fondle, gone, honest, lion, wrong, icon, long, among, hone, diphthong, pond, tong, Avon, soon, tone, won, yonder, son

141 142 143 144 145 146 147 148 149 150

Practice Sentences

1. My plane will arrive on time.
2. I hope to arrive early but may miss my ride.
3. The manager accepted the responsibility.
4. The man from Japan married a girl from America.
5. They moved to Korea.
6. My mother baked me some bread.
7. My home has three bedrooms.
8. He speaks quietly, but he is a liar.
9. I accept the responsibility.
10. He agreed the burden is great.
11. I saw horses and cows on the farm.
12. He is a very intelligent man.
13. He is very humble for a manager.
14. The assistant continued to disobey.
15. I traveled downtown on my mule.
16. They agreed to accept the responsibility.
17. We traveled by train to the goat farm.
18. We visited the Philippines and Japan.
19. I agree with the assistant.
20. The cows and sheep were calm.
21. Last night we went downtown.
22. A mule is not intelligent.
23. We went downtown to buy a mule.
24. I have an aunt and uncle who live on a farm.

New Signs List

Word	Synonym	Memory Aid	Sentence	Word	Synonym	Memory Aid	Sentence
accept	approve, approval	—	18	goats	—	chin, forehead	11
afternoon	—	—	12	honor	esteem	—	19
agree	—	*think - same*	15	humble	meek	—	20
almost	barely	—	6	intelligent	—	—	1
angry	wrath, anger	—	16	Japan	—	—	13
assistant	—	—	4	Korea	—	—	13
become	—	—	16	manager	master	—	4
bicycles	—	pedaling	12	multiplication	multiply, worse	—	7
burden	—	—	10	notice	—	—	17
bus	—	—	5	obey	—	—	9
calm	still, quiet	—	17	our	—	—	12
cannot	can't	—	19	Philippines	—	—	13
cow	—	—	11	plane	—	—	5
criticism	cancel, correct (papers)	—	18	poor	—	—	20
disagree	—	*think - opposite*	15	pressure	—	—	20
disobey	—	—	9	respect	—	—	19
do not	don't, not	—	18	responsibility	—	—	8
downtown	town	—	12	sheep	—	scissors cut wool	11
easily	simple	—	18	smart	—	—	1
easy	simple	—	7	things	—	—	15
farm	—	beard	11	train	—	tracks	5
fire	flames	—	6	—	—	—	—

Lesson 16

1.  **His**  **brother**
male + *same*
is **very**
BHA
[*V* hands]
 **proud**
pride

 of **him.**

2. **The**  **car**
BHA
drive
 **passed**
RHA / L→R
[R *A* hand passes L]

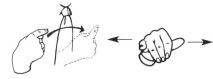 **us** **as** **if** **in** **a**
 race.
OUT / AA
compete, competition, contest

3. **If**
BHA / AA
[*F* hands, thumbs strike]
 you
 would
shall, will
 study
WF
 more,

you

could
can, able,
power

2X / BHA
succeed
accomplish, achievement,
effective
[do second time higher]

F→R
too!
also

4.

You

have
(possessive)

the

R-on-L
right
just, correct

R
idea!

5.

You

EA / 2X
should
need, have to,
ought, must

not
don't

WA
let
allow, may

your
(possessive)

R
imagination
imagine (verb)

BHA / AA
control
rule, reign,
master, manage

your
(possessive)

life.

6.

R-on-L
College
school + over

BHA
requires
requirement, insists,
requests, demands
(hooked forefinger)

you

to

memorize
mind - grasp

many

things.
F→R

7.

My
R-on-B
mine
[touch chest]

reason
cause, excuse
[*R* like *think*]

for
WA

telling
R
saying, speak

you

this
now,
here

is

to help
L-in-R

you.

8.

Do

you

have
(possessive)

any
→R
[*A* hand]

more

information ?
√ BHA / F→L   F-X
inform, notify

9.
√

Wait for
→L / WF
[L higher than R]

me

after
RL
across

church.
R-on-L
[*C* hand]

10.

I

have
(completed action)

visited
BHA / OUT / AA
[*V* hands]

√ →R
California,
earlobe + *yellow*

√ R-in-L
New York,
[*Y* in L palm]

√
New Jersey,

√
Chicago,
[*C* hand]

RHA / L→R
and

√
Detroit.
[*D* hand]

11.

I

F→R
also
too

BHA / OUT / AA
visited
[*V* hands]

√ R
Washington,
[*W* R shoulder out]

√ CW
D.C.,
[*D C* circled]

RHA / L→R
and

F→R
St. Louis.
STL

12.

While
during

R
there

I

BHA / OUT / AA
visited
[*V* hands]

the

√
Lincoln
[*L* on forehead]

√
Memorial.
remember

13.

I

√
believe
trust
[*mind* + *grasp*]

Lincoln
[*L* on forehead]

had
(possessive)

great
wonderful

principles.
[R *P* in L palm facing out]

14.

In
R-in-L

our

generation
BHA / AA / R→L

we

read
eyes scanning book

about
CW

divorces
WA
[*D* hands]

daily.
2X
[*A* brushes R cheek twice]

15.

In a few days

we

will
shall, would

begin
R-in-L / WA
start, instituted,
initially

regular
2X / R-on-L
consecutive, consistent
moves forward [*just* twice]

classes.
BHA
[*C* hands]

16.

A few days ago
yesterday + few

I

was

asked
F→B
pray

a **foolish** **question.**
silly, ridiculous
?

17. **It** **is**

a **wise** **person** **who** **does** **not**
R / 2X   personal   C-C-W   don't
             [P hands]

believe **in** **dreams.** **18.** **He**
trust   R-in-L   OUT / WF
mind + grasp   [R forehead]

was **stupid** **compared** **to** **his** **brother.**
[back of V on forehead] analogy   male + same
                         cupped hands

19. **I** **was** **surprised** **because**
                  eyes snap open

his   **idea** (R)   **was**   **judged**
decision, decided, determined
   best.

20.   **I**   **suspect**
suspicion [scratch forehead]
   he   **received**
R-O-L / IN

attention
horse blinders
2X
   because   **he**   **was**

so   **careless,**
reckless [*V* like *foolish*]
   strict,
WA
hard-nosed
   and
RHA / L →R
   cruel.
mean

Fingerspelling Practice Drills

("an" and "er" words)

another, antique, wander, sander, than, anthology, pander, either, neither, other, brother, German, mother

151 152 153 154 155 156 157 158 159 160

Practice Sentences

1. You memorized the information.
2. I was surprised he knew the question.
3. The foolish boy almost had an accident.
4. To succeed you need strict study habits.
5. I suspected something was wrong.
6. It surprised me when the man laughed.
7. The young man was careless.
8. We passed St. Louis, Missouri.
9. Is that information about Lincoln true?
10. I dreamed I went to California.
11. The reason he came was to compare ideas.
12. He was very proud of his sister.
13. She lost the information about the school.
14. Don't miss sign language class.
15. His imagination controlled his life.
16. I visited Chicago while on vacation.
17. There is much snow in New York.
18. I watched the sunset from the plane.
19. Yesterday my father had eggs and bacon.
20. We baked cookies yesterday for our class.
21. My mother asked the manager for a turtle.
22. My friend visited France.
23. My cousin accepts criticism well.
24. I was very careless with that glass.

New Signs List

Word	Synonym	Memory Aid	Sentence	Word	Synonym	Memory Aid	Sentence
a few days ago	—	yesterday + few	16	memorial	remember	—	12
attention	—	horse blinders	20	memorize	—	mind - grasp	6
because	—	—	19,20	more	—	—	3
believe	trust	mind + grasp	13	New Jersey	—	—	10
California	—	earlobe + yellow	10	New York	—	—	10
careless	reckless	—	20	passed	—	—	2
Chicago	—	—	10	principles	—	—	13
compared	analogy	cupped hands	18	proud	pride	—	1
control	rule, reign, master, manage	—	5	question	—	?	16
daily	—	—	14	received	—	—	20
Detroit	—	—	10	regular	consecutive, consistent	moves forward	15
divorces	—	—	14	requires	requirement, insists, requests, demands	—	6
dreams	—	—	17	St. Louis	—	STL	11
foolish	silly, ridiculous	—	16	strict	—	hard-nosed	20
generation	—	—	14	study	—	—	3
idea	—	—	4	stupid	—	back of V on forehead	18
imagination	imagine (verb)	—	5	succeed	accomplish, achievement, effective	—	3
in a few days	—	tomorrow + few	15	surprised	—	eyes snap open	19
information	inform, notify	—	8	suspect	suspicion	—	20
judged	decision, decided, determined	—	19	wait for	—	—	9
life	—	—	5	Washington, D.C.	—	—	11
Lincoln	—	—	12,13	wise	—	—	17

Lesson 17

1.

√

R-on-B
My
mine
[touch chest]

R-O-L
advice

to

him

was

R-in-L
to stop

√
deceiving
dealing under the table

poor

BHA / IN / EA / AA
people.
[*P* hands]

2.

His

√
R-O-L
influence
large *advice*

R-in-L
in

the

BHA
class
[*C* hands]

√
R-in-L
proved

he

√
didn't care.

3.

He

invented
[*4* hand up from forehead]

his

C-C-W
reason
cause, excuse

WA
for

missing
absent

BHA
class.
[*C* hands]

4.

I

guess
miss, estimate

he

is

C-C-W / EA
only
alone, someone

WA
crazy.
[*5* claw hand at
R ear rotated]

5.

She

became
[L in front R]

C-C-W
dizzy
[*5* claw hand
in front of eyes]

RL
after
across

he

kissed
mouth - cheek

her.

6.

It

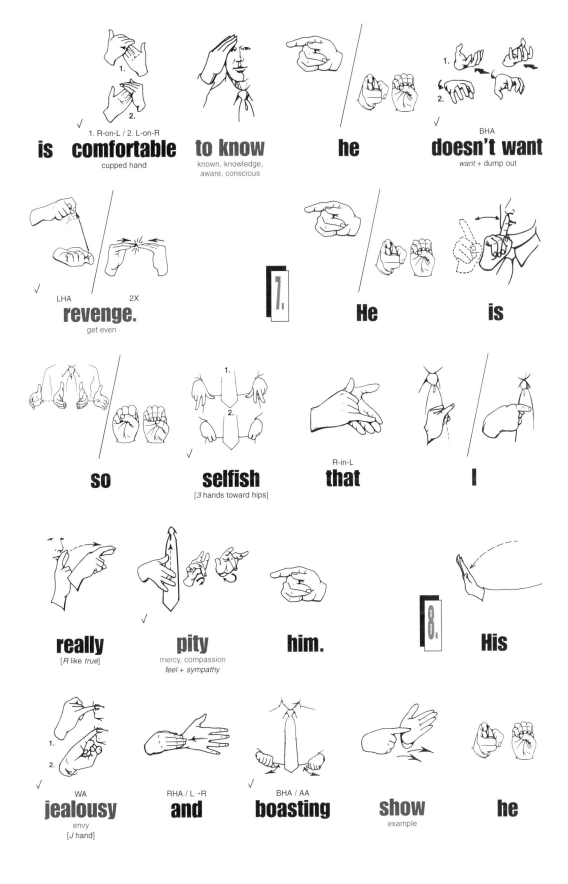

is **comfortable**

1. R-on-L / 2. L-on-R
cupped hand

to know

known, knowledge,
aware, conscious

he

doesn't want

BHA
want + dump out

revenge.

LHA   2X
get even

He

is

so

selfish

[*3* hands toward hips]

that

R-in-L

I

really

[*R* like *true*]

pity

mercy, compassion
feel + sympathy

him.

His

jealousy

WA
envy
[*J* hand]

and

RHA / L→R

boasting

BHA / AA

show

example

he

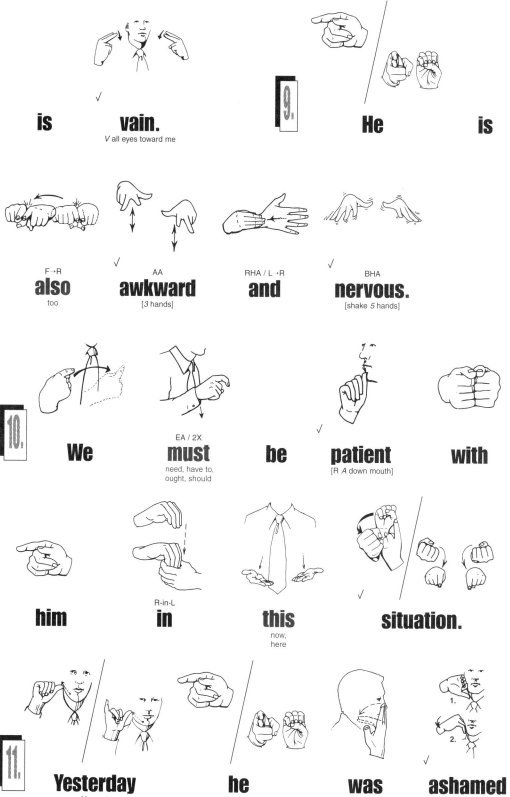

is   **vain.**

V all eyes toward me

9.

He   **is**

F→R
also
too

AA
awkward
[*3* hands]

RHA / L→R
and

BHA
nervous.
[shake *5* hands]

10.

We

EA / 2X
must
need, have to,
ought, should

be

patient
[R *A* down mouth]

with

him

R-in-L
in

this
now,
here

situation.

11.

Yesterday
Y - past

he

was

ashamed

1.

2.

RHA / L→R
and

embarrassed.
red and flushed face

12.

He

→L
causes

much
a lot of, amount
[comparative or quantity]

R-on-L
grief
crushed heart
[*A* hands]

RHA / L→R
and

suffering
agony
[*S* hands around each other]

to

his

BHA
mother.

13.

He

is

really
[*R* like *true*]

discouraged
depressed (2.)
heart drops

RHA / L→R
and

AA
cries
weep
tears flowing

because

he

is

R
lonely.

14.

I

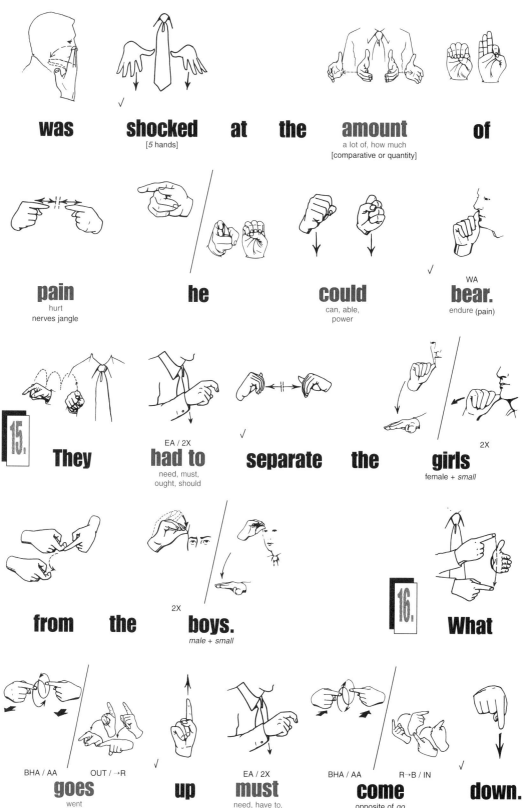

was   **shocked**   **at**   **the**   **amount**   **of**
[5 hands]

a lot of, how much
[comparative or quantity]

pain   **he**   **could**   WA
bear.
hurt
nerves jangle

can, able,
power

endure (pain)

They   **had to**   **separate**   **the**   **girls**
EA / 2X

need, must,
ought, should

2X

female + *small*

from   **the**   **boys.**   **What**
2X

male + *small*

goes   **up**   **must**   **come**   **down.**
BHA / AA   OUT / →R

went
opposite of *come*

EA / 2X

need, have to,
ought, should

BHA / AA   R→B / IN

opposite of *go*

17.

He   **stood**   **before**   **the**   **judge**

in front of, presence of,
presence

decision + person

RHA / L→R
and   **pleaded**   **innocent.**

2X
begged

[two *H's* on lips, then out]

18.

We

BHA / AA   OUT / →R
went   **out**   **of**   **town**   **ahead of**

go
opposite of *come*

[L *C* hand]

→R
downtown
rooftops

go on
[continue a discussion]

→R
the   **others.**   **19.**   **We**   **saw**   **him**

another

see

among   **the**   **people,**   **then**   **he**

BHA / IN / EA / AA

[*P* hands]

R
suddenly
quick, fast, immediate
shoot marble

disappeared.
vanished, solved problem

20.

I

was

R-in-L
in

the

R-in-L
center
middle
[*M* hand]

of

→R
town
downtown
rooftops

RHA   BHA
when

R-on-B
my
mine
[touch chest]

BHA
car
drive

R-in-L
stopped.

Fingerspelling Practice Drills

("ar" words)

army, armor, ark, bark, lark, lard, hard, card, guard, jar, car, mar, partner, far, war, ward, warden, barn, yard

161 162 163 164 165 166 167 168 169 170

Practice Sentences

1. The manager agreed with us.
2. The strongest animal on the farm is the mule.
3. A few days ago I had to memorize principles.
4. The advice he gave was selfish.
5. Accept my advice and don't be ashamed.
6. You need the right ideas to succeed.
7. She felt very ashamed; she was selfish.
8. The people were happy for the president.
9. He doesn't want everyone to know.
10. The job had a great influence on him.
11. I don't think he was deceiving me.
12. Mike was awkward while playing football.
13. The little boy was filled with jealousy.
14. Please loan me the new car seat.
15. Jealousy can become embarrassing.
16. He invented a new way to study.
17. My advice was not to be afraid.
18. He proved his innocence.
19. She was discouraged because of her grief.
20. Tom was discouraged by his awkwardness.
21. Mary pleaded with him to be patient.
22. She was very nervous and had a hard time.
23. The man said his car had vanished.
24. He continued his regular work.

New Signs List

Word	Synonym	Memory Aid	Sentence	Word	Synonym	Memory Aid	Sentence
advice	—	—	1	had to	must, need, should, ought	—	15
ahead of	go on	—	18	influence	—	large *advice*	2
among	—	—	19	innocent	—	—	17
ashamed	—	—	11	invented	—	—	3
awkward	—	—	9	jealousy	envy	—	8
bear	endure	—	14	judge	—	*decision* + person	17
became	—	—	5	kissed	—	mouth - cheek	5
before	in front of, presence of, presence	—	17	lonely	—	—	13
boasting	—	—	8	nervous	—	—	9
causes	—	—	12	others	another	—	18
center	middle	—	20	patient	—	—	10
comfortable	—	cupped hand	6	pity	mercy, compassion	*feel + sympathy*	7
crazy	—	—	4	pleaded	begged	—	17
deceiving	—	dealing under the table	1	proved	—	—	2
didn't care	—	—	2	revenge	get even	—	6
disappeared	vanished, solved problem	—	19	selfish	—	—	7
discouraged	depressed	heart drops	13	separate	—	—	15
dizzy	—	—	5	shocked	—	—	14
doesn't want	—	*want* + dump out	6	situation	—	—	10
down	—	—	16	suffering	agony	—	12
embarrassed	—	red and flushed face	11	then	—	—	19
grief	—	crushed heart	12	up	—	—	16
guess	miss, estimate	—	4	vain	—	*V* all eyes toward me	8

Lesson 18

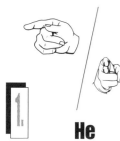

1.

He

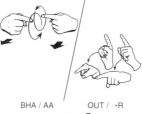

BHA / AA   OUT / →R
went
go
opposite of *come*

RL
across

the

street
way

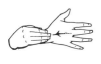

RHA / L →R
and

√
fell

√   R →L
against

a

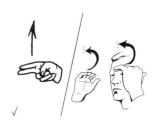

√
high

√
wall.

2.

We

believe
trust
mind + grasp

R-in-L
in

WF / BHA
life
alive

after
beyond

F →R
death.
dead
turn over

3.

Will
shall, would

you

R-on-B
please
like, enjoy, privilege,
appreciate, pleasure

R-in-L
lie down
[R *V* in L]

RHA / L→R
and

R-in-L
stop

R-on-L   F-X
jumping ?

4.

We

were
in past,
previously

at

a

BHA / WA
party
P + play

where

we

EA / 2X
had to
need, must,
ought, should

R-in-L
kneel
Protestant

all

the

R-on-L
time.
wristwatch

5.

Have

you

R / OUT
traveled
trip, journey

F-X
much ?
a lot of, amount
[comparative or quantity]

6.

While
during

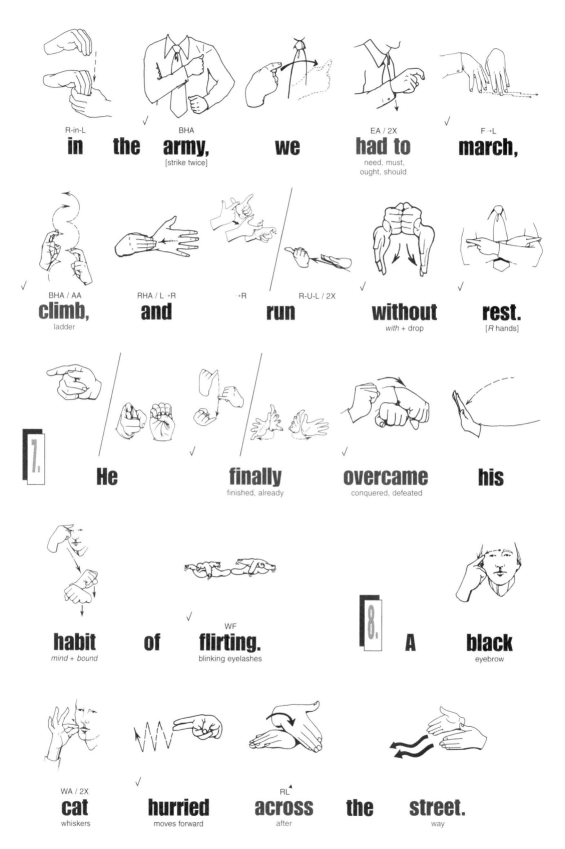

R-in-L
in **the**

BHA
army,
[strike twice]

we

EA / 2X
had to
need, must,
ought, should

F→L
march,

BHA / AA
climb,
ladder

RHA / L→R
and

→R
run

R-U-L / 2X

without
with + drop

rest.
[*R* hands]

7.

He

finally
finished, already

overcame
conquered, defeated

his

habit
mind + bound

of

WF
flirting.
blinking eyelashes

8.

A

black
eyebrow

WA / 2X
cat
whiskers

hurried
moves forward

RL
across
after

the

street.
way

9. **The** **clown**
large nose

F→R

led

the

→R / R-U-L

escape
flee, fled

attempt.
try
[*T* hands]

10. **We**

were

R

told
say, speak

to line up
[*5* hands]

RHA / L →R

and

→L / WF

wait for
[L higher than R]

the

R-on-L

train.
tracks

11. **It**

is

important
valuable, special

that

you

have
(possessive)

R-in-L

tickets.

12. 2X
The food
dine, eat

tasted

RHA / L →R

and

R / 2X

smelled

terrible,
awful, horrible

but
BHA / WA
however

he

was

polite.
2X
etiquette, proper
[like *fine*]

13.

As
while, during

I

touched
R-on-L

the

meat,
flesh

I

noticed
[from eye to L palm]

that

it

was

spoiled.
ruined

14. **The salesman**

was

trying
attempting
[*T* hands]

to impress
R-in-L / WA
emphasize

us

with

his

debating
WA / 2X
debate, discuss

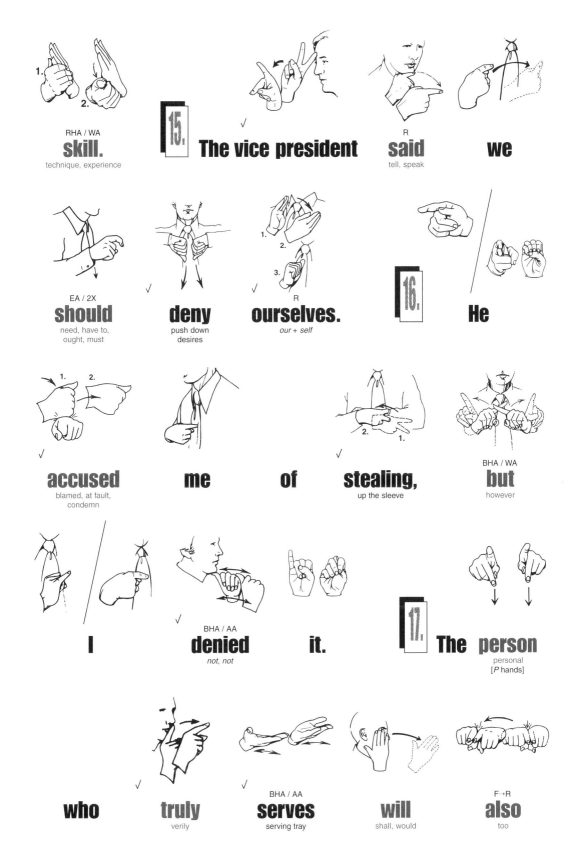

skill.
RHA / WA
technique, experience

15. ✓ **The vice president**

said
R
tell, speak

we

should
EA / 2X
need, have to,
ought, must

deny ✓
push down
desires

ourselves. ✓
R
our + self

16. **He**

accused ✓
blamed, at fault,
condemn

me

of

stealing, ✓
up the sleeve

but
BHA / WA
however

I

denied ✓
BHA / AA
not, not

it.

17. **The person**
personal
[*P* hands]

who

truly ✓
verily

serves ✓
BHA / AA
serving tray

will
shall, would

also
F→R
too

√
R-in-L
share

R-in-L
all

he

has.
(possessive)

18.

I

√
2X
warned

√
RHA
neither

√
champion

to

L →B
leave
left, depart

the

room.
[*R* hands]

19.
Are

√
RHA
either

of

you

√
willing

to

WA / 2X
debate

F-X
?
debating, discuss

20.
He

√
scattered

R-on-L / 2X
paper

√
while
during

mowing (the lawn).
blades moving

Fingerspelling Practice Drills

(mixed words)

house, yard, bus, zebra, fuss, going, whale, sky, trampoline, highway, school, couch

171 172 173 174 175 176 177 178 179 180

Practice Sentences

1. He denied it when accused of flirting.
2. The salesman quickly impressed them.
3. They tried to escape the lineup.
4. Army life is terrible for some people.
5. He was warned not to jump from the car.
6. The saleslady was very polite at home.
7. The army attempted to climb the high wall.
8. I noticed the food tasted terrible.
9. I warned him to stop stealing.
10. He accused her of stealing.
11. They warned us about the food.
12. The salesman tried to impress us.
13. The army lined up and marched.
14. The dizzy horse hit the manager.
15. He was discouraged when she became sick.
16. His advice greatly influenced the young man.
17. My cousin went in the store.
18. I saw a goat farm while traveling in Greece.
19. I felt sick yesterday.
20. I will ride in a train, airplane, and a boat.
21. The boy accused me of kissing him.
22. The preacher at my church went on vacation.
23. Let the Spanish children play.
24. Mother made cookies and an apple pie.

New Signs List

Word	Synonym	Memory Aid	Sentence	Word	Synonym	Memory Aid	Sentence
accused	blamed, at fault, condemn	—	16	line up	—	—	10
against	—	—	1	march	—	—	6
army	—	—	6	mowing	—	blades moving	20
attempt	try	—	9	neither	—	—	18
beyond	after	—	2	ourselves	—	*our + self*	15
champion	—	—	18	overcame	conquered, defeated	—	7
climb	ladder	—	6	polite	etiquette, proper	—	12
clown	—	large nose	9	rest	—	—	6
debating	debate, discuss	—	14,19	salesman	—	—	14
denied	—	*not, not*	16	scattered	—	—	20
deny	—	push down desires	15	serves	—	serving tray	17
either	—	—	19	share	—	—	1
escape	flee, fled	—	9	spoiled	ruined	—	13
fell	—	—	1	stealing	—	up the sleeve	16
finally	finished, already	—	7	tasted	—	—	12
flirting	—	blinking eyelashes	7	terrible	awful, horrible	—	12
high	—	—	1	tickets	—	—	11
hurried	—	moves forward	8	touched	—	—	13
important	valuable, special	—	11	truly	verily	—	17
impress	emphasize	—	14	vice president	—	—	15
jumping	—	—	3	wall	—	—	1
kneel	Protestant	—	4	warned	—	—	18
led	—	—	9	willing	—	—	19
lie down	—	—	3	without	—	*with + drop*	6

Lesson 19

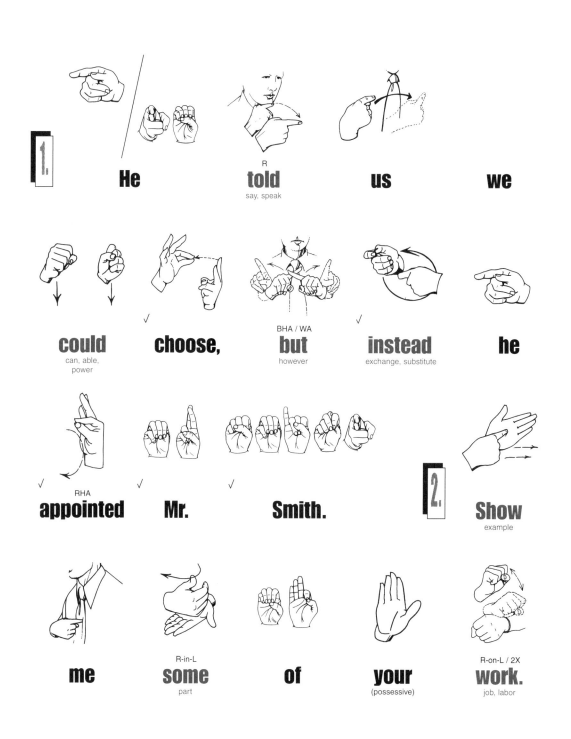

1.

He

told
say, speak

us

we

could
can, able,
power

choose,

but
BHA / WA
however

instead
exchange, substitute

he

appointed
RHA

Mr.

Smith.

2.

Show
example

me

some
R-in-L
part

of

your
(possessive)

work.
R-on-L / 2X
job, labor

3. **Show** **me** **an** BHA **example** **to** BHA / AA **explain**

example · · · describe · [F hands]

  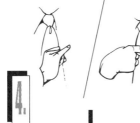 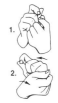

R-in-L · · · BHA · · · modified A hands

that. **4.** **I** **offered** **to** **change**

suggest, present · [modified A hands]

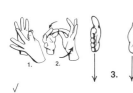 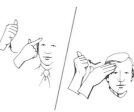 

interpreters **because** **of** **the** **vocabulary.**

[F hands] · · · [V like *word*]

5. **I** **volunteered** **to** **postpone** **the** **punishment.**

applied · put off, delay · 2X
(as for a job)

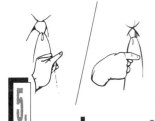  

6. **They** BHA **surrendered** **rather** R-on-L **than** **defend**

gave up, yielded · better · protect

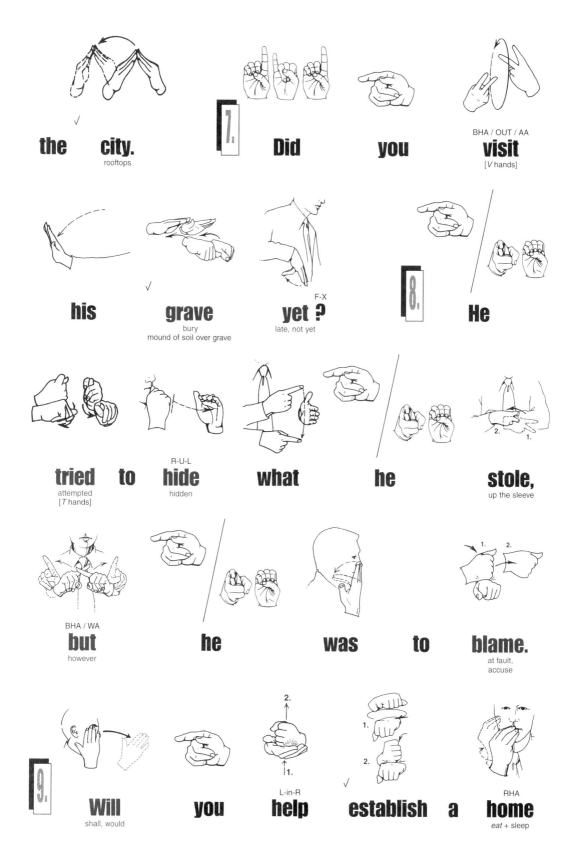

the **city.**
rooftops

7.

Did

you

BHA / OUT / AA
visit
[*V* hands]

his

grave
bury
mound of soil over grave

F-X
yet ?
late, not yet

8.

He

tried **to**
attempted
[*T* hands]

R-U-L
hide
hidden

what

he

stole,
up the sleeve

BHA / WA
but
however

he

was

to

blame.
at fault,
accuse

9.

Will
shall, would

you

L-in-R
help

establish

a

RHA
home
eat + sleep

WA
for

those

C-C-W
who

are

√
WA
tempted
temptation
elbow

to   **steal**   F-X
?
up the sleeve

I

don't
not

RHA
understand
recognize
light goes on

why
[*Y* hand]

they

have
(possessive)

the   L ›B
desire
long for, want,
wish

to steal.
up the sleeve

BHA / AA
If
[*F* hands,
thumbs strike]

you

WF
study

their

√
ways,
[*W* hands]

I

am

R
sure
true
[up and out from mouth]

you

can
could, able,
power

R-in-L
count
abacus

many

C-C-W
who
whom

fail.
[*V* off L palm]

12.

Did

you

graduate

from

CW   F-X
high school ?
[*H* + *S* circled]

13.

Your
(possessive)

RHA / WA
skill
experience, technique

at   **interpreting**
[*F* hands]

is

R-on-L
improving.
up arm

14.

His

R-on-L
sermon
lesson, message,
course, subject

was

so

expanded

R-in-L
that

it

needed
EA / 2X
must, have to,
ought, should

to be condensed.
abbreviated

I

15.

cannot
can't
[R forefinger hits L forefinger]

measure
BHA
[Y hands]

how much
a lot of, amount
[comparative or quantity]

he

earns.
R-in-L
deserves

16.

I

know
known, knowledge,
aware, conscious

he

spends
R-in-L
buys, purchases

all
R-in-L

the

money
R-in-L / 2X

he

borrows
R-on-L
[V hands in]

and
RHA / L →R

lends
R-on-L
[V hands out]

to

no
none

one.

17.

He **just** **cannot** **save**

can't
[R forefinger hits L forefinger]

R-on-L
store, reserve

R-on-L / OUT / 2X
enough
sufficient

R-in-L / 2X
money

WA
for

it.

18.

I **begged** **him** **to** **deliver**

2X
pleaded

√

L→R
bring, carry

the **newspaper** **free** **of** **charge.**

R-on-L / 2X
print
Linotype

√
[F hands]

√
cost, fine,
taxes

19.

The

group **voted** **to** **cooperate** **with** **the**

√
[G + class]

√
elected
ballot in box

√
gears mesh together

president.
superintendent

He

finally
last, final, end

✓
forbade
negative

✓
→R
anyone **to**

L→B
leave.
left, depart

Fingerspelling Practice Drills

("ah" words)

Dinah, Elijah, Jonah, Leah, Josiah, Judah, Korah

181 182 183 184 185 186 187 188 189 190

Practice Sentences

1. He will graduate from high school in June.
2. They postponed the punishment.
3. Don't blame the city for the situation.
4. He was appointed the city salesman.
5. He was forbidden to see the grave.
6. Mr. Campbell was appointed president.
7. Two interpreters quarreled.
8. He surrendered to his enemy last night.
9. We visited his grave last Saturday.
10. He was to blame for all the trouble.
11. I think my interpreting will improve.
12. I think you are dreaming about tomorrow.
13. You must rule your own life.
14. His wife spends his money before he earns it.
15. It is easy to postpone a job you don't like.
16. Our pastor postponed his sermon.
17. Anyone can be tempted to steal.
18. I failed the vocabulary test Friday at noon.
19. There were many graduates in high school.
20. Many people have to be begged to vote.
21. We looked at the bridge.
22. John broke the chair.
23. She offered me money for my shirt.
24. The Protestant began to sing and shout.

New Signs List

Word	Synonym	Memory Aid	Sentence	Word	Synonym	Memory Aid	Sentence
anyone	—	—	20	improving	—	up arm	13
appointed	—	—	1	instead	exchange, substitute	—	1
change	—	—	4	interpreters	—	—	4
charge	cost, fine, taxes	—	18	interpreting	—	—	13
choose	—	—	1	lends	—	—	16
city	—	rooftops	6	measure	—	—	15
condensed	abbreviated	—	14	Mr.	—	—	1
cooperate	—	gears mesh together	19	no	none	—	16
count	—	abacus	11	offered	suggest, present	—	4
defend	protect	—	6	postpone	put off, delay	—	5
deliver	bring, carry	—	18	punishment	—	—	5
earns	deserves	—	15	Smith	—	—	1
establish	—	—	9	spends	buys, purchases	—	16
expand	—	—	14	surrender	give up, yield	—	6
fail	—	—	11	tempted	temptation	elbow	9
forbade	negative	—	20	those	—	—	9
free	—	—	18	vocabulary	—	*V* like *word*	4
graduate	—	—	12	volunteered	applied (as for a job)	—	5
grave	bury	mound of soil over grave	7	vote	elect	ballot in box	19
group	—	—	19	ways	—	—	11
high school	—	—	12	—	—	—	—

Lesson 20

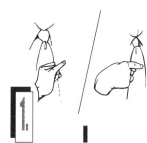 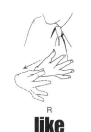 

I   R **like**   **him,**   BHA / WA **but** *however*   **you**

can't   ✓ R-on-L **depend on** *dependent*   **him.**   BHA / AA **If** [*F* hands, thumbs strike]

cannot [R forefinger hits L forefinger]

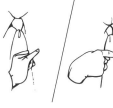  

I   EA / 2X **have to** need, must, ought, should   **I**   **will** shall, would

✓ RHA / OUT **force** [*C* forward]   **you**   R-in-L **to stop**   ✓ **teasing** slight *persecution*   **him.**

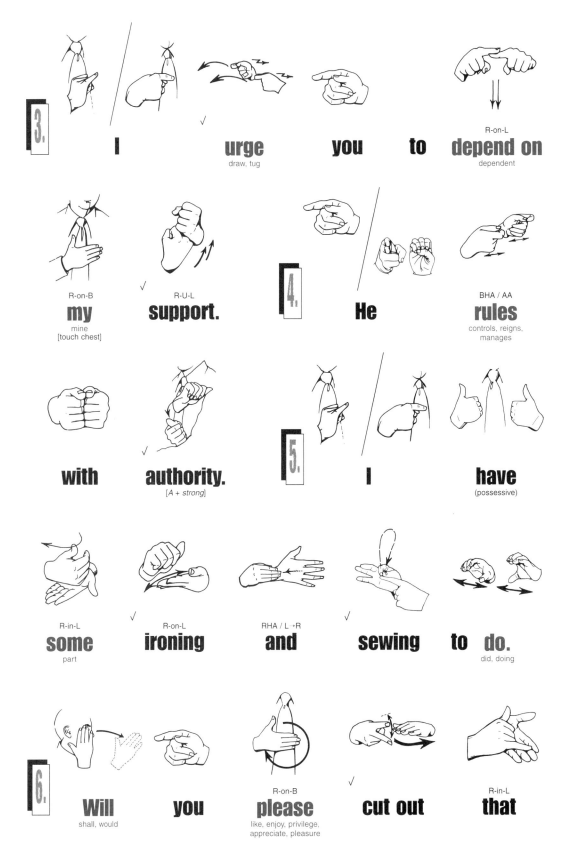

3.

I **urge** **you** **to** **depend on**
draw, tug | | | R-on-L
dependent

my **support.** **4.** **He** **rules**
R-on-B | R-U-L | | | BHA / AA
mine | | | | controls, reigns,
[touch chest] | | | | manages

with **authority.** **5.** **I** **have**
[A + strong] | | | (possessive)

some **ironing** **and** **sewing** **to** **do.**
R-in-L | R-on-L | RHA / L→R | | | did, doing
part

6. **Will** **you** **please** **cut out** **that**
shall, would | | R-on-B | | R-in-L
| | like, enjoy, privilege,
| | appreciate, pleasure

picture ?
[*C* hand]
F-X

1.

He

loves ✓

to hunt ✓
gun

and
RHA / L→R

fish ✓
casting rod

since ✓

he

retired. ✓
[*R*'s like *idle*]

8.

He

is

very
BHA
[*V* hands]

skilled
RHA / WA
experienced, technique

in
R-in-L

art. ✓
R-in-L
draw

9.

Soon
R-on-L
short, temporary

the

time
(age, historical)
[*T* hand]

of

reaping ✓
harvest

will
shall, would

be

over. ✓
completed

10.

He   is   **hard-of-hearing**
√   F→R

but
BHA / WA
however

lip-reads
√   C-C-W
speech-reads

better
rather

than
R-on-L

average.
R-on-L
medium, between

11.

He   **really**
[*R* like *true*]

has
(possessive)

a

good
R-in-L

voice.
√
[*V* up throat]

12.

Would
shall, will

you

please
R-on-B
like, enjoy, privilege,
appreciate, pleasure

make
R-on-L
made

the

announcements
√
announce, proclaim

now
here,
this

?
F-X

13. She has a bad habit
(possessive) WA mind + bound

of gossiping. ✓ BHA

14. I command ✓ order large *tell*

you to stop doing that.
R-in-L ✓ BHA R-in-L

15. I told them not
R say, speak don't

to whisper in class. **16.** I
✓ 2X R-in-L BHA [*C* hands]

promised **not** **to scold** **him** **any**

✓ R-on-L   don't   ✓   →R
                                [A hand]

more. **They** **shouted** **and**

screamed
[C up]

RHA / L →R

mocked **the** **tall** **hired** **man.**

✓ →L   ✓ RHA   ✓ R →B
made fun of

I **wrote** **a** **letter** **to**

R-in-L

the **radio** **station.** **The** **clouds**

✓   ✓   L→R / BHA / C-C-W

are

BHA
dark

today
now + day

with

√
R-O-L / R-U-L
thundering

RHA / L →R
and

√
lightning.

We

BHA / AA
walked
steps

R-in-L
in **the** **valley**

RHA / L→R
and

then

BHA / AA
climbed
ladder

our

√
own

√
mountain.
rock + hill

Fingerspelling Practice Drills

("th" words)

Seth, Ruth, Nathan, Nathaniel, Thomas, Abiathar, Matthew, Goliath, Elizabeth, Jethro, Esther, Timothy, Dathan

191 192 193 194 195 196 197 198 199 200

Practice Sentences

1. Please let me have your attention.
2. I have visited Chicago and California.
3. Can you lip-read or do you mock the person?
4. He has a teasing voice and whispers a lot.
5. He shouted in the valley when he arrived.
6. Lightning struck the radio announcer.
7. The retired preacher loves to fish and hunt.
8. Success is promised to those who lip-read.
9. The average voice can whisper and shout.
10. The valley is full of apples.
11. Larry will force John to obey the rules.
12. Sue has to iron and sew some shirts.
13. The time of reaping in Illinois has arrived.
14. People should use their voices at the game.
15. He promised not to gossip.
16. She disobeyed the rules so she was scolded.
17. The thunder over the mountains was terrible.
18. She teased him in a whispering voice.
19. He depends on hunting for food for dinner.
20. The lightning forced us to go home.
21. The promise about the program was broken.
22. They mocked the command to start the hunt.
23. Sewing is a beautiful skill.
24. There was lightning on the mountain.

New Signs List

Word	Synonym	Memory Aid	Sentence	Word	Synonym	Memory Aid	Sentence
announce-ments	proclaim, announce	—	12	over	completed	—	9
art	draw	—	8	own	—	—	20
authority	—	—	4	promised	—	—	16
command	order	large *tell*	14	radio	—	—	18
cut out	—	—	6	reaping	harvest	—	9
depend on	dependent	—	1,3	retired	—	—	7
doing	—	—	14	scold	—	—	16
fish (verb)	—	casting rod	7	sewing	—	—	5
force	—	—	2	since	—	—	7
gossiping	—	—	13	station	—	—	18
hard-of-hearing	—	—	10	support	—	—	3
hired	—	—	17	tall	—	—	17
hunt	—	gun	7	teasing	—	slight *persecution*	2
ironing	—	—	5	thundering	—	—	19
lightning	—	—	19	urge	draw, tug	—	3
lip-reads	speech-reads	—	10	valley	—	—	20
loves	—	—	7	voice	—	—	11
mocked	made fun of	—	17	whisper	—	—	15
mountain	—	*rock + hill*	20	—	—	—	—

Lesson 21

1.

BHA / AA   R→B
Coming
opposite of *go*

R-in-L
back
again

we

BHA / AA
walked
steps

√   **along**   **the**   √   **sea**
→R
ocean,
waves

√   **shore.**
2X
[tip of R hand to
tip of L twice]

2.

Will
shall, would

you

√
C-C-W
take care
keep

of   **the**

√   **grass**
grow + green

RHA / L→R
and

R→L
flowers

R-in-L
in

R-on-B
my
mine
[touch chest]

√
→L / 2X
garden
hoeing

F-X
?

3.

He

✓
subtracted
omitted, take away

my
mine
[touch chest]

✓
share

of

the

profits.
money in watch
pocket

4. **What** **percent** **did** **he** **pay**
WA / R-in-L

you **after**
RL
across

they ✓ **divided** **the** **farm** **?**
L→R   F-X
beard
[5 hand under chin]

5. **He** **looks**
WA
appears,
seems

very
BHA

✓ **thin**
thin cheeks

now.
this,
here

6. **He** **is** **a** ✓ **famous**
small *announcements*

person /
personal
[*P* hands]

R-in-L   R-on-B   R-in-L

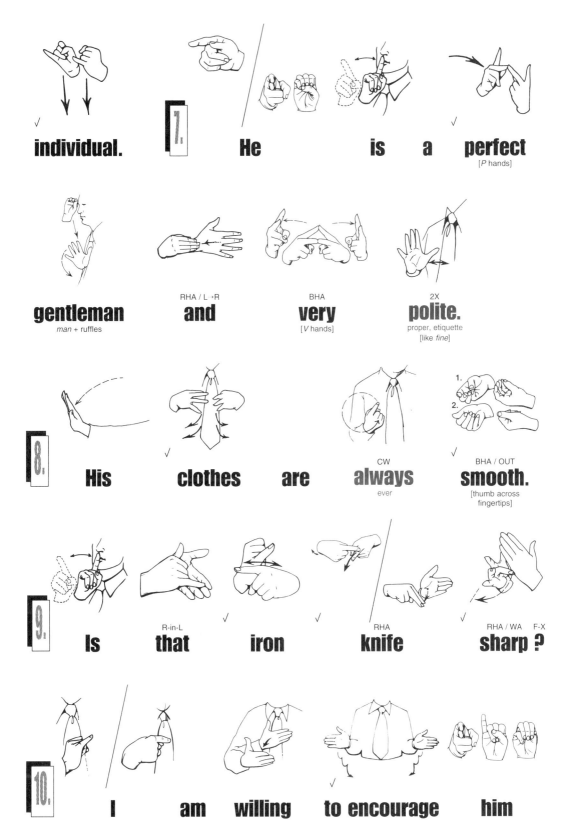

individual.

7.

He   **is**   **a**   **perfect**
[*P* hands]

gentleman
man + ruffles

RHA / L →R
and

BHA
very
[*V* hands]

2X
polite.
proper, etiquette
[like *fine*]

8.

His   **clothes**   **are**
CW
always
ever

BHA / OUT
smooth.
[thumb across
fingertips]

9.

Is
R-in-L
that   **iron**
RHA
knife
RHA / WA   F-X
sharp ?

10.

I   **am**   **willing**   **to encourage**   **him**

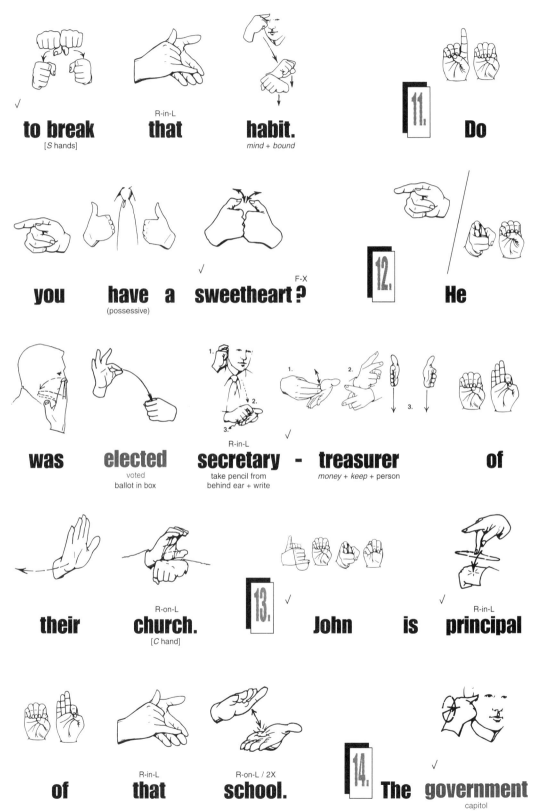

to break
[S hands]

R-in-L
that

habit.
mind + bound

11. **Do**

you

have a
(possessive)

sweetheart ?
F-X

12. **He**

was

elected
voted
ballot in box

R-in-L
secretary -
take pencil from
behind ear + write

treasurer
money + keep + person

of

their

R-on-L
church.
[C hand]

13. **John**

is

R-in-L
principal

of

R-in-L
that

R-on-L / 2X
school.

14. **The** **government**
capitol

requires **us** **to pay** **taxes.**

BHA

requirement, insists,
requests, demands

WA / R-in-L

cost, charge,
fine

15. **Did** **you** **see** **the** **king** **and**

saw

K - royalty

RHA / L→R

queen ? **16.** **The** **prince** **looked at** **his**

F-X

Q - royalty

P - royalty

look for,
watch for

robe **in** **the** **mirror.** **17.** **He**

R-in-L

is **an** **officer** **in** **the** **Russian** **army.**

official

R-in-L

BHA / 2X

[strike twice]

18.

He **served**
serving tray

during **the** **Korean**
while

BHA / AA

BHA

War.
battle
[4 hands]

BHA / AA

19.

They **called** **the** **police**
phone
[C or 5 claw hand]

after **the** **accident.**
across
[A hands]

RL

20.

A **nurse**
[N at pulse]

came **with** **the** **doctor** **to check**
physician
[D at pulse]

BHA / AA / R→B

his **bones.**

Practice Sentences

1. The doctor was a policeman in that town.
2. Did the government need you during the war?
3. Be careful; he has a sharp knife in his hand.
4. The principal of that school had an accident.
5. Will you divide the flowers among the class?
6. The doctor's nurse was a sweetheart too!
7. His neighbor's friend had a new secretary.
8. The king was polite to all.
9. The farmer was a famous person in Germany.
10. The flowers on the farm were beautiful.
11. The king and queen are very famous.
12. My garden did not give much profit.
13. He showed us his grandfather's grave.
14. He is hard-of-hearing but can ride horseback.
15. He checked the electricity.
16. The machine counted our money.
17. The program at the school was very good.
18. His voice sounded like a horse.
19. He retired and now is skilled in acting.
20. The girl begged the man to give her bread.
21. The president lends all our money.
22. I try but cannot measure God's love.
23. Did you see the new car at school?
24. My mother loves children and animals.

New Signs List

Word	Synonym	Memory Aid	Sentence	Word	Synonym	Memory Aid	Sentence
along	—	—	1	perfect	—	—	7
bones	—	—	20	police	—	—	19
break	—	—	10	prince	—	*P - royalty*	16
check	—	—	20	principal	—	—	13
clothes	—	—	8	profits	—	money in watch pocket	3
divided	—	—	4	queen	—	*Q - royalty*	15
doctor	physician	—	20	robe	—	—	16
encourage	—	—	10	Russian	—	—	17
famous	—	small *announcements*	6	sea	ocean	waves	1
garden	—	hoeing	2	share (noun)	—	—	3
government	capitol	—	14	sharp	—	—	9
grass	—	*grow + green*	2	shore	—	—	1
individual	—	—	6	smooth	—	—	8
iron	—	—	9	subtracted	omitted, take away	—	3
king	—	*K - royalty*	15	sweetheart	—	—	11
knife	—	—	9	take care of	—	*keep*	2
Korean	—	—	18	thin	—	thin cheeks	5
mirror	—	—	16	treasurer	—	*money + keep + person*	12
nurse	—	—	20	war	battle	—	18
officer	official	—	17	—	—	—	—

Lesson 22

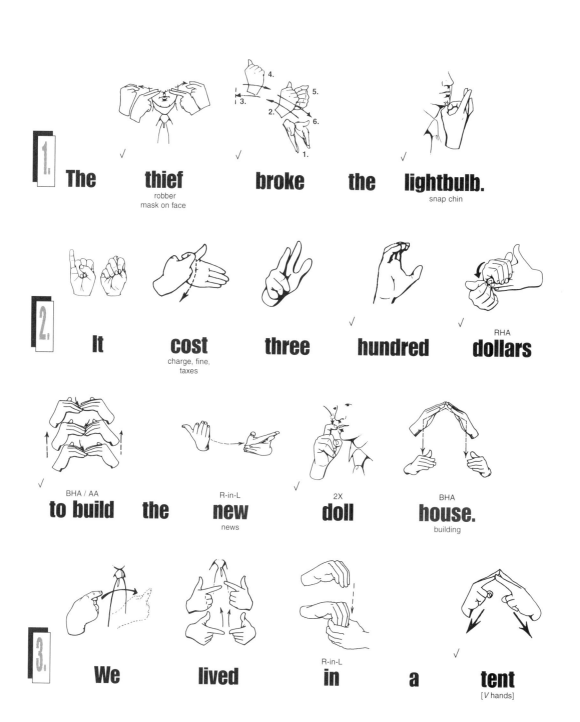

1.

The   thief   broke   the   lightbulb.

robber
mask on face

snap chin

2.

It   cost   three   hundred   dollars

charge, fine,
taxes

RHA

BHA / AA   R-in-L   2X   BHA

to build   the   new   doll   house.

news   building

3.

We   lived   in   a   tent

R-in-L

[*V* hands]

during
while

F→R
camp
two tents

meeting.
service, gathering

4.

She

F→R
put
place

RHA / WF
candles

R-on-L
on

the

R-in-L
cake.
hot cross buns

5.

Did

you

L→R
bring
carry

your
(possessive)

R-on-L / RHA   F-X
umbrella ?

6.

Did

you

C-C-W / R-on-L
wash
[*A* hands]

with

R-in-L / 2X   F-X
soap ?

7.

I

EA / 2X
need
must, have to,
ought, should

a

RHA / WA
knife,

R-in-L
fork,

RHA / L →R
and

2X
spoon.

8.

He

forgot
wipe from mind

his

toothbrush.

9.

Paul

→R / R-U-L
escaped
flee, fled

by

CW
using
[*U* circled]

a

basket
wastebasket, trash,
garbage

RHA / L →R
and

a

BHA / WA
rope.
[← *R* fingers →]

10. **A**

thread
wire, string
[← *I* fingers →]

was

tied
tie a bow

to

the

BHA / WA
rope.
[← *R* fingers →]

11.

He

√
lost **the** **buttons** **off** **his** **coat.**
[*A* hands down lapels]

12. **He** **became** **broke** **when**
BHA / WA
[L in front R, twist]
√
RHA   BHA

√
RHA
fired.   **13.**   **I**   **heard** **the**
listen
[*C* at R ear]

√
BHA
wedding **was** **beautiful.** **14.** **He**
[R hand in L]
C-C-W
pretty, lovely,
beauty

√   √   F →R / BHA
gave **her** **a** **diamond** **as** **an**
[*D* at ring finger]

√
engagement
[E at L ring finger]

R-on-L
ring.
[R hand]

15.

I

had
(possessive)

→R
another
other

√
engagement /
lock, reservation

R-on-L
appointment

so

I

could
can, able,
power

not
don't

BHA / AA   OUT / →R
go.
went
opposite of *come*

16.

He

has
(possessive)

a

R-on-L
nice
clean

√   C-C-W
personality
[P over L chest, circled]

RHA / L→R
and

a

R
fine
[5 hand]

√
character.
characteristic
[C like personality]

17.

R-on-B
My
mine
[touch chest]

glasses

cost
charge, fine,
taxes

two dollars

RHA / L→R
and

ten cents.
penny + ten

18.

R-on-B
Please
like, enjoy, privilege,
appreciate, pleasure

L→R
take

this
now,
here

R-in-L
list

of

R-in-L
rules
[*R* hand]

with

you.

19.
The

foundation
support to L arm

of

the

BHA
building
house

is

BHA
very
[*V* hands]

R-in-L
weak.

20.
The

hospital

is

an

R-on-L
institution
[*I* hand]

of

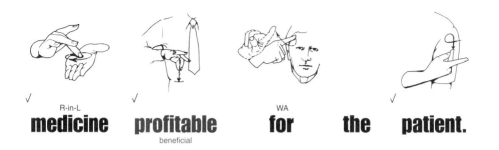

√   √   WA   √

R-in-L

medicine   **profitable**   **for**   **the**   **patient.**

beneficial

Practice Sentences

1. She lost the diamond from her wedding ring.
2. He had a terrible personality.
3. Don't forget to bring your glasses.
4. The doctor told him to go to the hospital.
5. The buttons on my coat cost $1.10.
6. Every institution has a list of rules.
7. The thief sold the ring for ten cents.
8. The sewing basket is full of old buttons.
9. The famous Korean nurse was a sweetheart.
10. The Russian officer was very thin.
11. Please take care of the garden.
12. She washed the umbrella with soap.
13. She forgot to bring a knife, fork, and spoon.
14. We brought the basket to the game.
15. Her diamond engagement ring was beautiful.
16. Joe was told the cost of the ring.
17. The building is on a strong foundation.
18. The hospital was very expensive.
19. We forgot our coat and toothbrushes.
20. It is raining, so bring your umbrella.
21. We learned the rules of the game from Jack.
22. He brought his new black glasses to work.
23. She enjoyed her engagement ring.
24. The book went into the basket.

New Signs List

Word	Synonym	Memory Aid	Sentence	Word	Synonym	Memory Aid	Sentence
appointment	—	—	15	institution	—	—	20
basket	wastebasket, trash, garbage	—	9	lightbulb	—	snap chin	1
broke	—	—	1	list	—	—	18
broke (money)	—	—	12	lost (lose)	—	—	11
build (verb)	—	—	2	medicine	—	—	20
buttons	—	—	11	off	—	—	11
camp	—	two tents	3	patient (person)	—	—	20
candles	—	—	4	Paul	—	—	9
cents (10)	—	*penny + ten*	17	personality	—	—	16
character	characteristic	*C* like *personality*	16	profitable	beneficial	—	20
diamond	—	—	14	rope	—	—	9
doll	—	—	2	rules (list of)	—	—	18
dollars	—	—	2	soap	—	—	6
engagement	—	—	14	spoon	—	—	7
engagement (appointment)	lock, reservation	—	15	tent	—	—	3
fired	—	—	12	thief	robber	mask on face	1
fork	—	—	7	thread	wire, string	—	10
foundation	—	support to L arm	19	tied	—	tie a bow	10
gave	—	—	14	toothbrush	—	—	8
glasses (eye)	—	—	17	umbrella	—	—	5
hospital	—	cross on L shoulder	20	wedding	—	—	13
hundred	—	—	2	—	—	—	—

Lesson 23

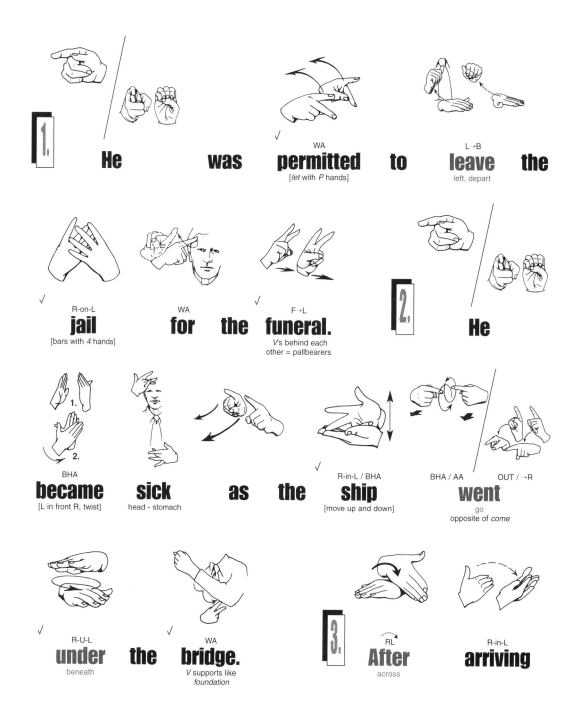

1.

He   **was**   ✓ WA **permitted**   **to**   L→B **leave**   **the**
[*let* with *P* hands]   left, depart

✓ R-on-L **jail**   WA **for**   **the**   ✓ F→L **funeral.**   **2.**   **He**
[bars with *4* hands]   *V*s behind each other = pallbearers

BHA **became**   **sick**   **as**   **the**   ✓ R-in-L / BHA **ship**   BHA / AA   OUT / →R **went**
[L in front R, twist]   head - stomach   [move up and down]   go opposite of *come*

✓ R-U-L **under**   **the**   ✓ WA **bridge.**   **3.**   RL **After**   R-in-L **arriving**
beneath   *V* supports like *foundation*   across

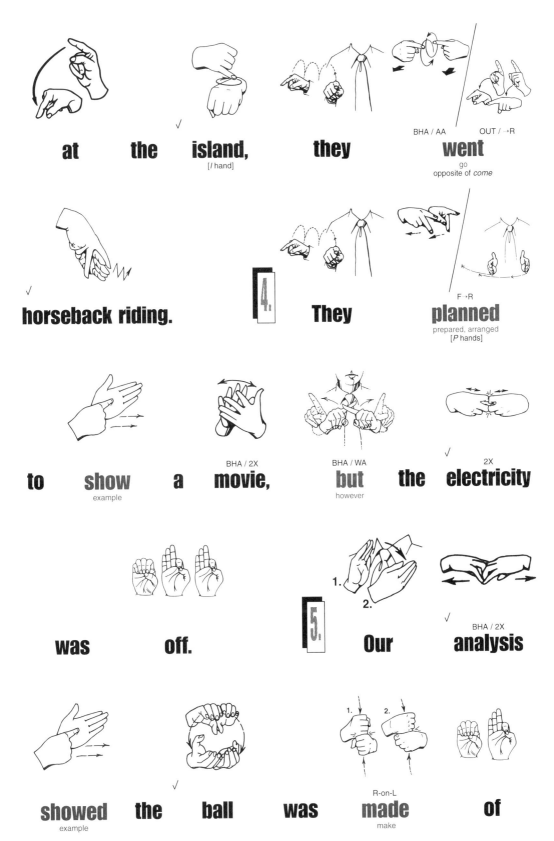

at　　**the**　　**island,**
[/ hand]

they

BHA / AA　　OUT / →R
went
go
opposite of *come*

✓
horseback riding.

4.　**They**

F →R
planned
prepared, arranged
[*P* hands]

to　　**show**　　**a**　　**movie,**
example　　　　BHA / 2X

BHA / WA
but
however

the

✓　　2X
electricity

was　　**off.**

5.　**Our**

✓　BHA / 2X
analysis

showed
example

the　　**ball**　　**was**

R-on-L
made
make

of

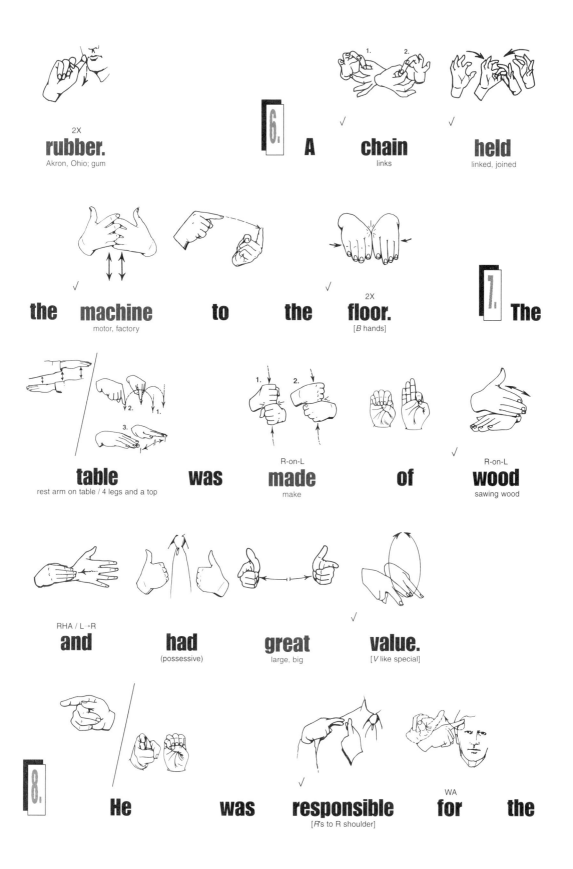

2X
rubber.
Akron, Ohio; gum

6.

A

√
chain
links

√
held
linked, joined

√
the

machine
motor, factory

to

√
the

2X
floor.
[*B* hands]

7. **The**

table
rest arm on table / 4 legs and a top

was

R-on-L
made
make

of

√ R-on-L
wood
sawing wood

RHA / L→R
and

had
(possessive)

great
large, big

√
value.
[*V* like special]

8.

He

was

√
responsible
[*R*s to R shoulder]

WA
for

the

√
poem,
P + song

√
R-in-L
which
that

was

read.
eyes scanning book

9.
The

R-in-L
new
news

√
→R
equipment
E + thing

√
R-in-L
developed
[D hand]

his

√
energy.
E + strong

10.
The

√
R-on-L
normal
nation, national

person
personal
[P hands]

will
shall, would

√
R-on-L / 2X
function
[F hand]

√
1.   2.
maturely.
1. *M + full*
2. *M + tall*

11.
R-on-B
My
mine
[touch chest]

√
BHA
reaction
[R hands]

was

that

the

√
R-on-L
metal
[M hand]

was

√
R-on-L
reliable.
[R hands]

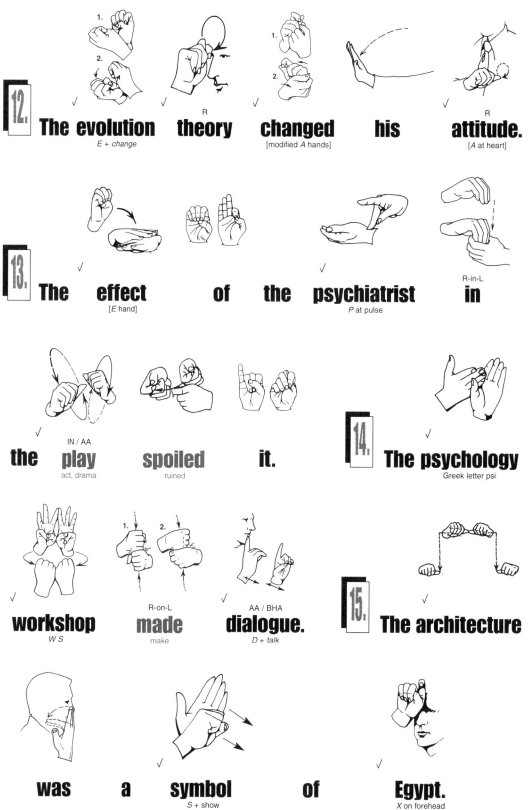

12. **The evolution**
E + change

theory
R

changed
[modified *A* hands]

his

attitude.
R
[*A* at heart]

13. **The** **effect**
[*E* hand]

of **the** **psychiatrist**
P at pulse

in
R-in-L

the **play**
IN / AA
act, drama

spoiled
ruined

it.

14. **The psychology**
Greek letter psi

workshop
W S

made
R-on-L
make

dialogue.
AA / BHA
D + talk

15. **The architecture**

was **a** **symbol**
S + show

of **Egypt.**
X on forehead

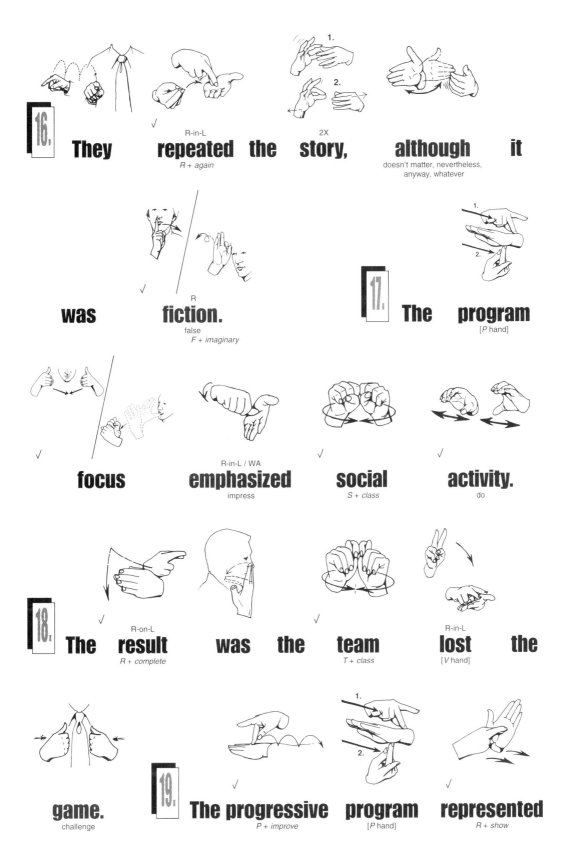

16.

They **repeated** **the** **story,** **although** **it**

R-in-L
R + again

2X

doesn't matter, nevertheless,
anyway, whatever

was **fiction.**

R
false
F + imaginary

17.

The **program**
[*P* hand]

focus **emphasized** **social** **activity.**

R-in-L / WA
impress

S + class

do

18.

The **result** **was** **the** **team** **lost** **the**

R-on-L
R + complete

T + class

R-in-L
[*V* hand]

game.
challenge

19.

The progressive **program** **represented**

P + improve

[*P* hand}

R + show

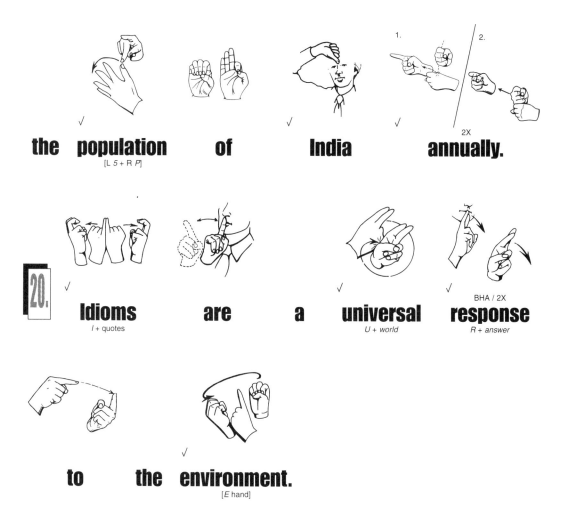

the population **of** **India** **annually.**
[L 5 + R P] 2X

20. **Idioms** **are** **a** **universal** **response**
I + quotes U + world R + answer
BHA / 2X

to **the** **environment.**
[E hand]

Practice Sentences

1. Lesson planning is important for teaching.
2. One of the symbols of love is kindness.
3. He prefers going home by ship.
4. There was no electricity on the island.
5. The workshop had no electricity.
6. The story was from a fiction book.
7. The play was about Egypt.
8. She is a psychiatrist.
9. They are responsible for the tables and chairs.
10. His poems greatly impressed them.
11. He was sick after he received the letter.
12. The machine doesn't work.
13. Did you get permission to travel with us?
14. Mary has been visiting a psychiatrist.
15. His dialogue was difficult to sign.
16. The evolution theory is an imaginary idea.
17. Those metal machines are reliable.
18. Egypt was represented at the meeting.
19. The funeral in India had a deep effect.
20. The psychologist noticed the man's attitude.
21. Their response was different.
22. The rubber ball rolled under the table.
23. The architecture of the bridge is beautiful.
24. We were permitted to ride horseback.

New Signs List

Word	Synonym	Memory Aid	Sentence	Word	Synonym	Memory Aid	Sentence
activity	do	—	17	maturely	—	*M + full; M + tall*	10
analysis	—	—	5	metal	—	—	11
annually	—	—	19	normal	nation, national	—	10
architecture	—	—	15	permitted	—	—	1
attitude	—	—	12	play	act, drama	—	13
ball	—	—	5	poem	—	*P + song*	8
bridge	—	*V* supports like foundation	2	population	—	—	19
chain	—	links	6	progressive	—	*P + improve*	19
developed	—	—	9	psychiatrist	—	*P* at pulse	13
dialogue	—	*D + talk*	14	psychology	—	Greek letter psi	14
effect	—	—	13	reaction	—	—	11
Egypt	—	*X* on forehead	15	reliable	—	—	11
electricity	—	—	4	repeated	—	*R + again*	16
energy	—	*E + strong*	9	represented	—	*R + show*	19
environment	—	—	20	response	—	*R + answer*	20
equipment	—	*E + thing*	9	responsible	—	—	8
evolution	—	*E + change*	12	result	—	*R + complete*	18
fiction	false	*F + imaginary*	16	ship	—	—	2
floor	—	—	6	social	—	*S + class*	17
focus	—	—	17	symbol	—	*S + show*	15
function	—	—	10	team	—	*T + class*	18
funeral	—	*V*s behind each other = pallbearers	1	theory	—	*T + reason*	12
held	linked, joined	—	6	under	beneath	—	2
horseback riding	—	—	3	universal	—	*U + world*	20
idioms	—	*I + quotes*	20	value	—	—	7
India	—	—	19	which	that	—	8
island	—	—	3	wood	—	sawing wood	7
jail	—	—	1	workshop	—	*W S*	14
machine	motor, factory	—	6	—	—	—	—

Lesson 24

√

1. **The** **price** **of** **the** **dictionary** **was**

P + cost

EA / 2X

[R D in L palm]

√

√

plenty. **2.** **I** **guess** **we**

overflowing *miss, estimate*

EA / 2X √ R-in-L

must **paraphrase** **that** **poem.** **3.** **The**

need, have to, *P + change* *P + song*
ought, should

BHA / 2X √

teacher **represented** **the** **residential school** **authority.**

R + show *[I hand]* *A + strong*

4.

He **is** **the** **exact** **example**
[*F* hands]   BHA
                    E + show

of **a** **mule.**
          R
        donkey, stubborn

5. **I**

admit **I** **am** **no** **expert**
confess   none   RHA / WA
                                        [*F* at chin]

in **algebra.** **6.** **I** **wish**
R-in-L   *A* hands + *arithmetic*   L→B
                                               long for, desire,
                                                    want

to substitute **another** **course.** **7.** **I**
exchange, instead of   →R   R-on-L
               other   subject, lesson,
                      sermon, message

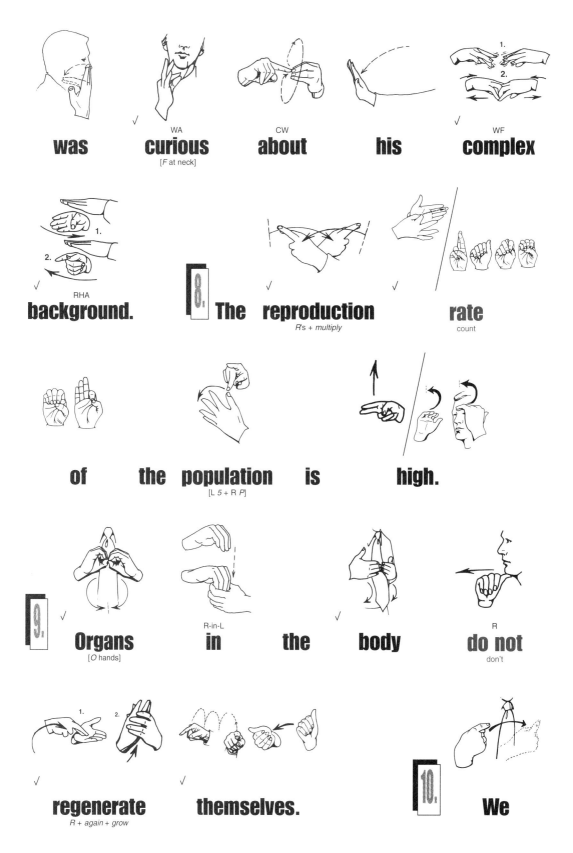

was **curious** **about** **his** **complex**

WA
[*F* at neck]

CW

WF

background. **The** **reproduction** **rate**

RHA

R's + multiply

count

of **the** **population** **is** **high.**

[*L 5 + R P*]

Organs **in** **the** **body** **do not**

[*O hands*]

R-in-L

R

don't

regenerate **themselves.** **We**

R + again + grow

will
shall, would

evaluate
AA
E's + *judging*

our

registration
register

techniques.
RHA / WA
skill, experience

11. **It** **is** **all right**
rights (civil)
to **demonstrate**
D + *show*
emotion.
E + *feel*

12. **I** **asked**
F→B
prayed
him **to** **abbreviate**
condense

his **report.**
[*R* at L wrist]

13. **The** **Coke**
[R at L arm]
[thumb moves]
advertisement
2X
commercial
trumpeting

illustration
I + *show*
was **cute.**
2X
[*H* on chin]

14. **The** **drama**
IN / AA
act, play

was   **a**   **boring**
dry under chin

disappointment.
miss (as in miss someone who is gone)
[*R* on chin]

15. ✓ **Congratulations** **on** **applying**
praise, applause
[clap hands]

WA
for

R-in-L
that

✓ **correspondence**
BHA / 2X

course.
R-on-L
sermon, message,
lesson, subject

16. **He**

put
F→R
placed

the

✓ **copy**
conform

of   **the**   **picture**
[*C* hand]

on
R-on-L

the

door.
RHA

17. **He**

cannot
can't
[R forefinger hits left forefinger]

BHA / AA
communicate

R-in-L
well.
good

18.
She

C-C-W / EA
only
alone, someone

added

to

his

disappointment.
miss (as in miss someone who is gone)

19.
The

RHA
sugar
sweet
[down mouth]

BHA
dissolved
D + disappeared

R-in-L
in

the

1.   2.
pop.
soda

20.
They

R-on-L / 2X
functioned
[F hand]

like
[Y hands]

professional
P + straight

BHA / IN / EA / AA
people
[P hands]

RHA / L →R
and

BHA
sued

him.

Practice Sentences

1. John admitted he is a Coke drinker.
2. Jane couldn't find the paper.
3. Larry is a curious, professional, boring man.
4. I am an expert on college registration.
5. Did you abbreviate your vocabulary?
6. She was ugly after the accident.
7. She comes from a residential school.
8. That is a complex algebra problem.
9. The drama had emotion but was boring.
10. He had a Coke with a cute girl.
11. I was curious about the regeneration rate.
12. The poem needed to be abbreviated.
13. She communicated like a professional.
14. They could not communicate.
15. Please demonstrate your new techniques.
16. The classes all had substitute teachers.
17. The algebra class disappointed everyone.
18. Algebra is complex when applied to prices.
19. He admitted he was curious about the girl.
20. Her disappointment showed in her emotions.
21. The advertisement was canceled by letter.
22. The course was evaluated by an expert.
23. Congratulations on completing the course.
24. The price of the dictionary was plenty.

New Signs List

Word	Synonym	Memory Aid	Sentence	Word	Synonym	Memory Aid	Sentence
added	—	—	18	emotion	—	E + feel	11
admit	confess	—	5	evaluate	—	E's + judging	10
advertisement	commercial	trumpeting	13	expert	—	—	5
algebra	—	A hands + arithmetic	5	illustration	—	I + show	13
all right	rights (civil)	—	11	like (same)	—	—	20
applying	—	—	15	organs	—	—	9
background	—	—	7	paraphrase	—	P + change	2
body	—	—	9	plenty	—	overflowing	1
Coke	—	—	13	pop	soda	—	19
communicate	—	—	17	price	—	P + cost	1
complex	—	—	7	professional	—	P + straight	20
congratula-tions	praise, applause	—	15	rate	—	count	8
copy	conform	—	16	regenerate	—	R + again + grow	9
correspon-dence	—	—	15	registration	register	—	10
curious	—	—	7	report	—	—	12
cute	—	—	13	reproduction	—	R's + multiply	8
demonstrate	—	D + show	11	residential school	—	—	3
dictionary	—	—	1	sued	—	—	20
disappoint-ment	miss	—	14,18	themselves	—	—	9
dissolved	—	D + disappeared	19	—	—	—	—

Lesson 25

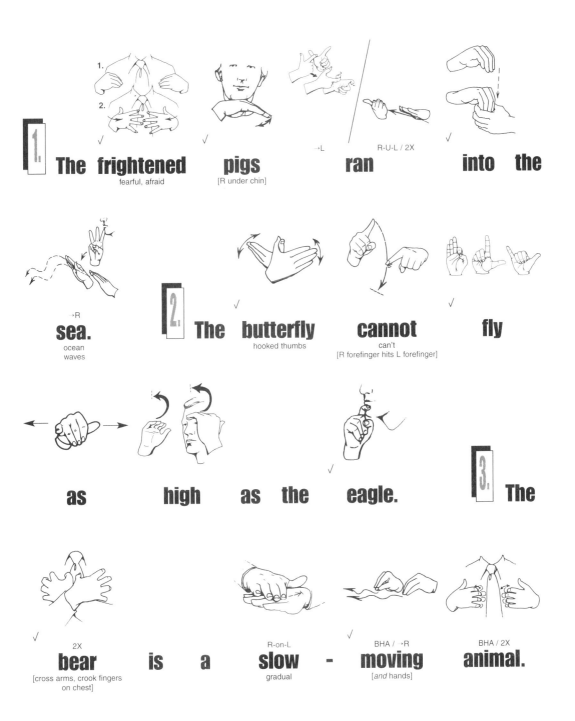

1. The **frightened** **pigs** **ran** **into** **the**
fearful, afraid
[R under chin]
→L   R-U-L / 2X

sea. **2.** The **butterfly** **cannot** **fly**
ocean   hooked thumbs   can't
waves   [R forefinger hits L forefinger]
→R

as **high** **as** **the** **eagle.** **3.** The

bear **is** **a** **slow** - **moving** **animal.**
[cross arms, crook fingers   gradual   [and hands]
on chest]   R-on-L   BHA / →R   BHA / 2X
2X

4.

RHA
Neither **the** **blind** **lion** **nor**
mane over head

the **wolf** **played** **together.** **5.** **Africa**
nose WA C-C-W / BHA RHA / C-C-W
[Y hands] with, circled [A hand}

is **well** **-** **known** **for** **monkeys.**
know, knowledge, WA scratch
aware, conscious

6. **He** **kills** **worms,** **bees,**
RHA RHA
[wiggle across L hand] [F at cheek]

flies, **and** **spiders.** **7.** **He**
[catching on arm] RHA / L→R [hook little fingers
and crawl]

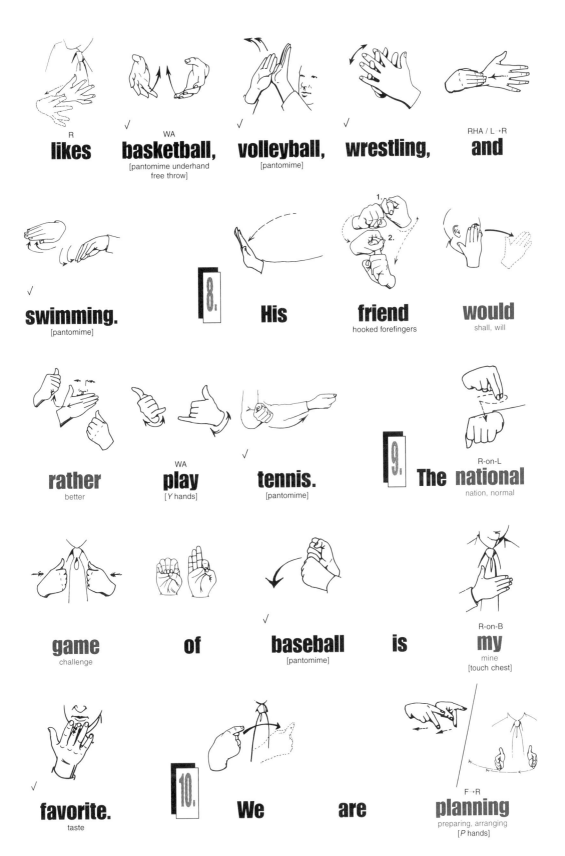

R
likes

WA ✓
basketball,
[pantomime underhand free throw]

✓
volleyball,
[pantomime]

✓
wrestling,

RHA / L→R
and

✓
swimming.
[pantomime]

8.

His

friend
hooked forefingers

would
shall, will

rather
better

WA
play
[*Y* hands]

✓
tennis.
[pantomime]

9.

The **national**
R-on-L
nation, normal

game
challenge

of

✓
baseball
[pantomime]

is

my
R-on-B
mine
[touch chest]

✓
favorite.
taste

10.

We

are

planning
F→R
preparing, arranging
[*P* hands]

a   **trip**
R / OUT
travel, journey
   to   **visit**
BHA / OUT / AA
[V hands]
   the   ✓ **country**
C-C-W
[Y at L elbow]
   of

✓ **Sweden.**
[S at forehead]
   11. **Last**
past, ago
   year   **we**

visited
BHA / OUT / AA
[V hands]
   ✓ **Norway,**
C-C-W
[N at forehead]
   ✓ **Denmark,**
C-C-W
[D at forehead]
   and
RHA / L→R
   ✓ **Finland.**
C-C-W
[F at forehead]

12. **He**   **came**
BHA / AA
opposite of go
R→B
   to   **the**   ✓ **U.S.**
CW

from   ✓ **China.**
WA
[forefinger at R eye]
   13. **He**   **is**

an   **American**   **Indian.**   **14.**   **One**

student
1. *study,*
2. & 3. *person* ending

WF

came
opposite of *go*

BHA / AA   R ·B

from

Malaysia
for dance

AA

and

RHA / L ·R

two   **from**   **Jamaica.**
island

RHA

15.   **In**

R-in-L

Mexico
[*M* on R cheek]

the

people
[*P* hands]

BHA / IN / EA / AA

speak
tell, say

R

Spanish.
Spain

BHA

16.   **He**   **likes**   **Ping-Pong**   **but**

RHA   [pantomime]   BHA / WA
however

loses
[V hand]

at

bowling.
[pantomime]

17. ✓ **Snakes** **are**
fangs

dangerous **pets.**
danger

18. ✓ **Rabbits** **are**

BHA
very
[V hands]

R
fast.
quick, sudden,
immediate

19. R-on-B
My
mine
[touch chest]

BHA
father

has
(possessive)

several
few

R
horses.

20. F→R
The **children**
child
[pats heads of children]

were

2X
shy
bashful, timid
[cupped hand brushes cheek]

of **the** **camels.**

Practice Sentences

1. I enjoy baseball, basketball, and bowling.
2. Sweden is famous for making movies.
3. The frightened Indian ran from the lion.
4. The swimming team came from Mexico.
5. Every morning she is like a bear to get up.
6. Pigs enjoy eating and sleeping.
7. The children were frightened by the pigs.
8. I would rather play basketball than tennis.
9. We visited Africa and saw the monkeys.
10. The spiders from Mexico are very dangerous.
11. The U.S. team defeated the Swedish team.
12. The eagle and rabbit were bothered by flies.
13. The lion and monkey don't eat worms.
14. The man was from the country of China.
15. Several bees frightened the Jamaican players.
16. The pigs were frightened by the butterfly.
17. Do they play baseball in China?
18. We had horses, pigs, and cows on our farm.
19. When I was in Sweden I played tennis.
20. He fell off the chair.
21. Her favorite colors were red and purple.
22. The tie cost them ten dollars.
23. He asked her to wait for him after class.
24. I suspect the population will expand.

New Signs List

Word	Synonym	Memory Aid	Sentence	Word	Synonym	Memory Aid	Sentence
American	—	—	13	lion	—	mane over head	4
baseball	—	—	9	Malaysia	—	for dance	14
basketball	—	—	7	Mexico	—	—	15
bear	—	—	3	monkeys	—	scratch	5
bees	—	—	6	moving	—	—	3
blind	—	—	4	nor	—	—	4
bowling	—	—	16	Norway	—	—	11
butterfly	—	hooked thumbs	2	pigs	—	—	1
camels	—	—	20	Ping-Pong	—	—	16
China	—	—	12	rabbits	—	crossed wrists	18
country	—	—	10	several	few	—	19
dangerous	danger	—	17	shy	bashful, timid	—	20
Denmark	—	—	11	snakes	—	fangs	17
eagle	—	—	2	spiders	—	—	6
favorite	—	taste	9	Sweden	—	—	10
Finland	—	—	11	swimming	—	—	7
flies	—	catching on arm	6	tennis	—	—	8
fly (verb)	—	—	2	two	—	—	14
frightened	fearful, afraid	—	1	U.S.	—	—	12
Indian	—	—	13	volleyball	—	—	7
into	—	—	1	wolf	—	nose	4
Jamaica	—	island	14	worms	—	—	6
kills	—	—	6	wrestling	—	—	7

Lesson 26

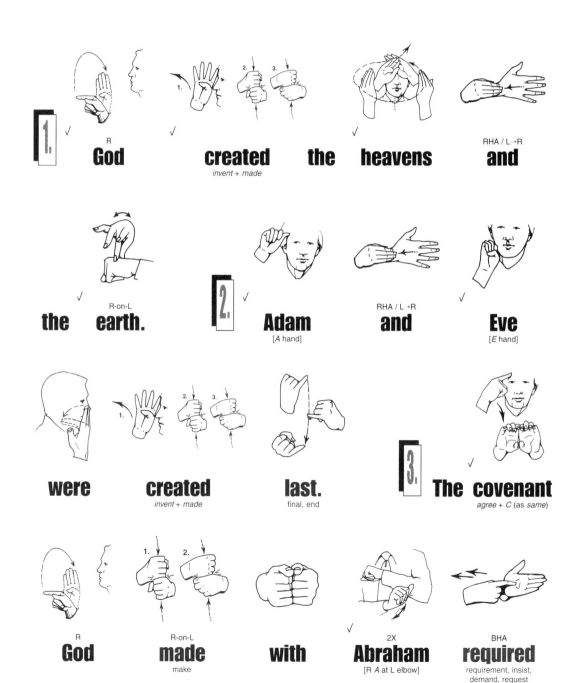

1. ✓ **God**
R

✓ **created**
invent + made

the

✓ **heavens**

and
RHA / L→R

✓ **the** **earth.**
R-on-L

2. ✓ **Adam**
[*A* hand]

and
RHA / L→R

✓ **Eve**
[*E* hand]

were **created**
invent + made

last.
final, end

3. ✓ **The covenant**
agree + C (as same)

God
R

made
R-on-L
make

with

✓ **Abraham**
2X
[*R A* at *L* elbow]

required
BHA
*requirement, insist,
demand, request*

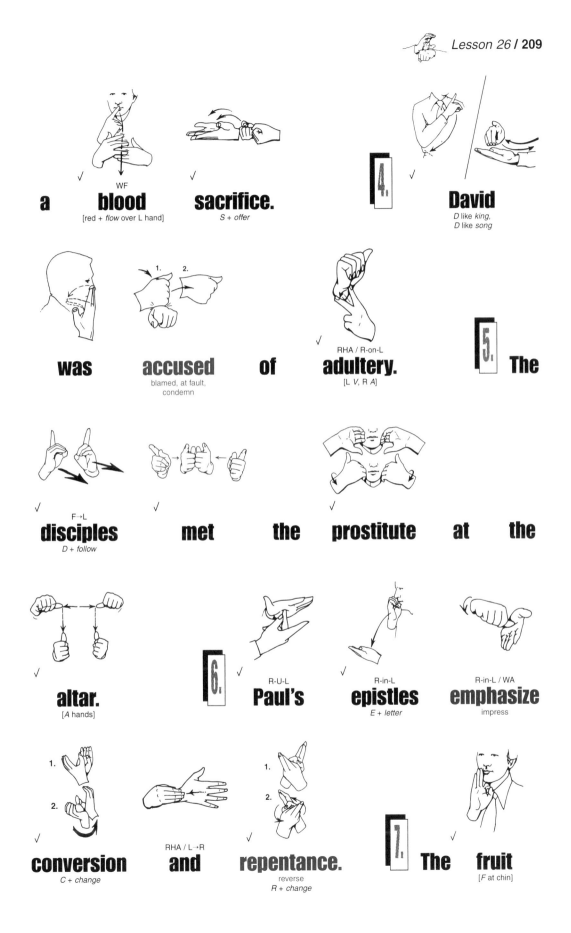

a   **blood**
[red + *flow* over L hand]

sacrifice.
S + offer

4.   **David**
D like *king*,
D like *song*

was   **accused**
blamed, at fault,
condemn

of   **adultery.**
RHA / R-on-L
[L *V*, R *A*]

5.   **The**

disciples
F→L
D + follow

met   **the**   **prostitute**   **at**   **the**

altar.
[*A* hands]

6.   **Paul's**
R-U-L

epistles
R-in-L
E + letter

emphasize
R-in-L / WA
impress

conversion
C + change

and
RHA / L→R

repentance.
reverse
R + change

7.   **The**   **fruit**
[*F* at chin]

of   **the**   **Spirit**
ghost, soul

is   **love,**   **joy,**
2X
happiness

and
RHA / L→R

peace.
R-in-L

Wicked
W + bad

men

crucified
[nail - hammer, then R
and outstretched arms]

Jesus
R-in-L / L-in-R
nail prints

at

Calvary.
rock + mountain + cross

The

gospel
2X
[G in L hand]

emphasizes
R-in-L / WA
impress

that

Jesus
R-in-L / L-in-R
nail prints

is

Messiah.
M + royalty

Moses
BHA

celebrated
anniversary,
hosanna

Passover

with **his** **people.**
BHA / IN / EA / AA
[*P* hands]

11. **The** **Jewish**
2X
goatee

rabbi
[*R*'s down chest]

was

√ **in charge of**
controls, reigns,
rules, manages

the

√ **temple.**
T + church

12. **The** **kingdom**
king + land, soil

of

R
God

is

no
none

√ R
myth.

13. **His**

√ WA
testimony
lecture, speech

of

the √ **miracle**
wonderful + work

was **a** √ **blessing.**
blessed
[*A* hands]

14.

I

preach
EA / 2X
F + lecture

√ **nothing**
*none + open
5 hands*

√ **except**
special, but

R-in-L / L-in-R
Jesus
nail prints

√ **Christ.**
R
C + royalty

15.

My
R-on-B
mine
[touch chest]

√ **religion**
R
[*R* at heart, down and out]

believes
trust
mind + grasp

in
R-in-L

√ **divine**
R-in-L
D + clean

healing
BHA
whole, well,
healthy

by

√ **faith.**
confidence
mind grasps

16.

√ **Christians**
Christ + person
Jesus + person

or

who
C-C-W
whom

√ **backslide**
[R *A* backs away from L *A*]

√ **lose**

their

√ **crown.**
[R&L thumb and center fingers
grasp crown and put on head]

17. **The**

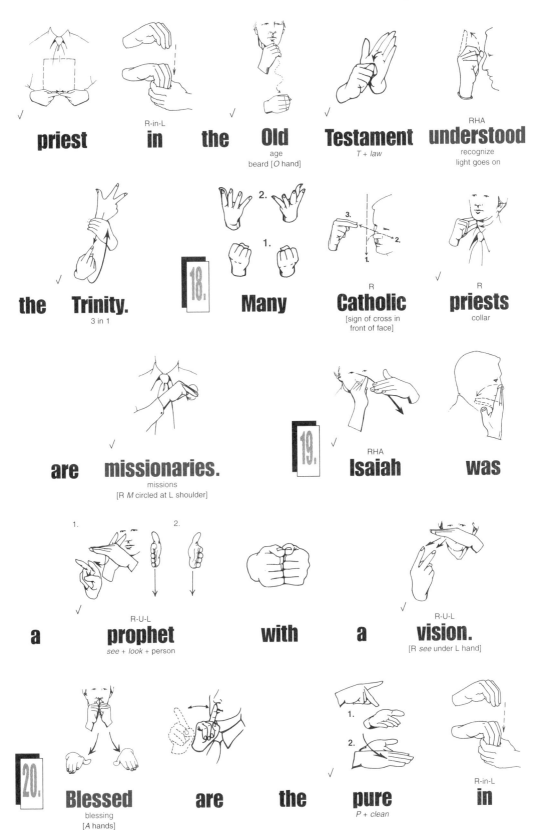

√
priest

in
R-in-L

√
the

√
Old
age
beard [O hand]

√
Testament
T + law

understood
RHA
recognize
light goes on

√
the

√
Trinity.
3 in 1

18. **Many**

Catholic
R
[sign of cross in
front of face]

√
priests
R
collar

√
are

missionaries.
missions
[R M circled at L shoulder]

19. √
Isaiah
RHA

was

√
a

prophet
R-U-L
see + look + person

with

a

√
vision.
R-U-L
[R see under L hand]

20. **Blessed**
blessing
[A hands]

are

the

√
pure
P + clean

in
R-in-L

√

heart
[draw heart on L chest]

RHA / L→R
and

√
mind;

they

are

not
don't

ashamed.

Practice Sentences

1. Jesus is our sacrificial Lamb.
2. Saul and Peter saw the same vision.
3. Jesus walked the valley of death alone.
4. The Messiah died on Calvary.
5. The Lamb of God is our blood sacrifice.
6. David was in charge of the armies.
7. Faith without works is dead.
8. The letters of Paul are in the New Testament.
9. Jesus was crucified so we could live forever.
10. Eve sinned when she ate the fruit.
11. They had sacrifices in the Old Testament.
12. Isaiah preached with a vision.
13. The kingdom is peaceful.
14. It was a miracle healing.
15. We visited the old temple.
16. Abraham had much faith.
17. David kept his heart and mind on God.
18. The prophets were often persecuted.
19. Christians will have crowns in heaven.
20. The Catholic priest prayed at the altar.
21. Abraham's covenant is a blessing.
22. God blesses His children.
23. Christ, our Messiah, is coming soon.
24. The disciples were followers of Christ.

New Signs List

Word	Synonym	Memory Aid	Sentence	Word	Synonym	Memory Aid	Sentence
Abraham	—	—	3	joy	happiness	—	7
Adam	—	—	2	kingdom	—	king + land, soil	12
adultery	—	—	4	lose	—	—	16
altar	—	—	5	Messiah	—	M + royalty	9
backslide	—	—	16	met	—	—	5
blessing	blessed	—	13	mind	—	—	20
blood	—	—	3	miracle	—	wonderful + work	13
Calvary	—	rock + mountain + cross	8	missionary	missions	—	18
celebrated	anniversary, hosanna	—	10	Moses	—	—	10
Christ	—	C + royalty	14	myth	—	—	12
Christians	—	Jesus + person, Christ + person	16	nothing	—	none + open, 5 hands	14
conversion	—	C + change	6	Old Testament	—	—	17
covenant	—	agree + C (as same)	3	Passover	—	—	10
created	—	invent + made	1,2	Paul's	—	—	6
crown	—	—	16	peace	—	—	7
crucified	—	—	8	preach	—	F + lecture	14
David	—	D like king; D like song	4	priest (O.T.)	—	—	17
disciples	—	D + follow	5	priest (Catholic)	—	collar	18
divine	—	D + clean	15	prophet	—	see + look + person	19
earth	—	—	1	prostitute	—	—	5
epistles	—	E + letter	6	pure	—	P + clean	20
Eve	—	—	2	rabbi	—	—	11
except	special, but	—	14	religion	—	—	15
faith	confidence	mind grasps	15	repentance	reverse	R + change	6
fruit	—	—	7	sacrifice	—	S + offer	3
God	—	—	1	spirit	ghost, soul	—	7
gospel	—	—	9	temple	—	T + church	11
heart	—	—	20	testament	—	T + law	17
heavens	—	—	1	testimony	lecture, speech	—	13
in charge of	controls, rules, reigns, manages	—	11	trinity	—	3 in 1	17
Isaiah	—	—	19	vision	—	—	19
Jesus	—	nail prints	8,9,14	wicked	—	W + bad	8

Lesson 27

Those **who**
C-C-W

trespass
break + law

God's
R

laws
R-in-L

are

evil.
R
E + bad

Acts

chapter
R-in-L
[C down L hand]

one

verse
R-on-L
Scripture
[across L palm]

eleven
[palm toward body]

recorded
R-on-L
applied

the

ascension
RHA
stand + ascend

of

Jesus.
R-in-L / L-in-R
nail prints

John

spoke
R
say, tell

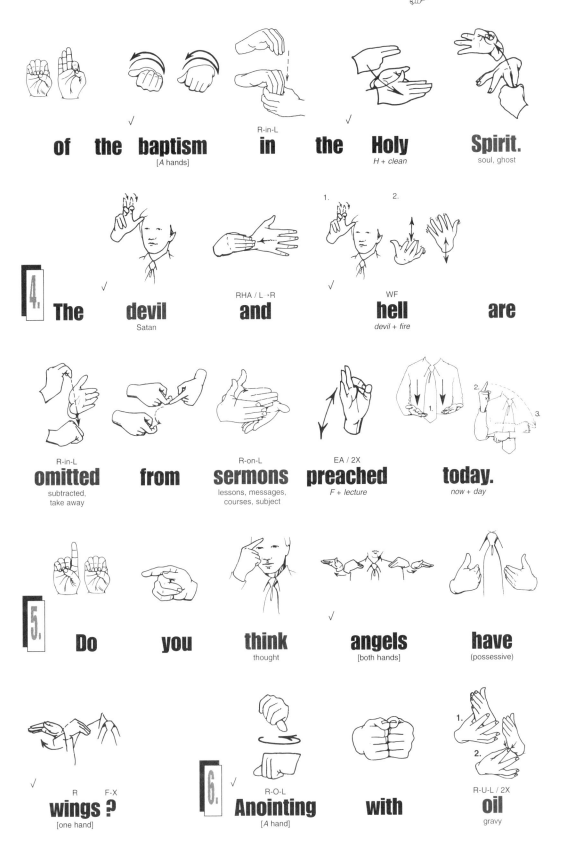

√
of **the** **baptism**
[*A hands*]

R-in-L
in **the** √ **Holy** **Spirit.**
H + clean   soul, ghost

4.
√   RHA / L→R   √   WF
The **devil** **and** **hell** **are**
Satan   devil + fire

R-in-L   R-on-L   EA / 2X
omitted **from** **sermons** **preached** **today.**
subtracted,   lessons, messages, F + lecture   now + day
take away   courses, subject

5.
√
Do **you** **think** **angels** **have**
thought   [both hands]   (possessive)

√   R   R-O-L   R-U-L / 2X
wings ?   6. √ **Anointing** **with** **oil**
[one hand] F-X   [*A hand*]   gravy

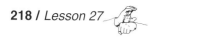

 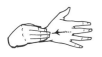   

RHA / L→R
and

praying
asking

WA
for

the

sick
head - stomach

is

✓

R-on-L
scriptural.
verse
[across L palm]

7. The

✓

Bible
Jesus book

✓

2X
warns
[R hits L]

R→L
against

✓

worshiping
adore

✓

images
[*A* hands]

or

✓

idols.
[*I* hands]

   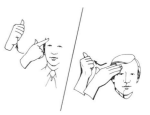

8. The

BHA / IN / EA / AA
people
[*P* hands]

disobeyed

the

✓

WA
Ten
[10]

✓

Commandments.
C + law

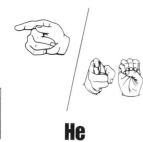 

9.

He

was

✓

R / 2X
convicted
guilty
heart jabbed

because

he

did not
don't

pay
WA / R-in-L

tithes.
R
1/10

10.

We

went
BHA / AA   OUT / →R
go
opposite of *come*

to

the

Presbyterian
R-in-L
[*P* hand]

church
R-on-L
[*C* hand]

at

Christmas
WA
[*C* hand]

and
RHA / L→R

Easter.
WA
[*E* hands]

11.

The

Mennonite
prayer bonnet ties

lady
woman + ruffles

had
(possessive)

a

Lutheran
R-in-L
[*L* hand]

husband.
man + married

12.

The

denominational
denomination

Protestant
R-in-L
kneeling

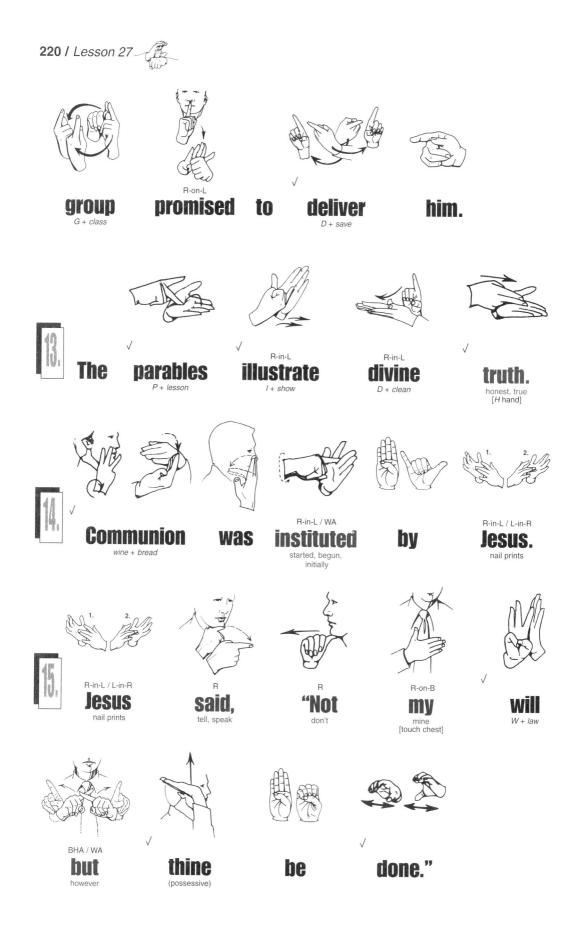

group
G + class

promised
R-on-L

to

deliver
D + save

him.

13. **The** **parables**
P + lesson

illustrate
R-in-L
I + show

divine
R-in-L
D + clean

truth.
honest, true
[H hand]

14. **Communion**
wine + bread

was

instituted
R-in-L / WA
started, begun,
initially

by

Jesus.
R-in-L / L-in-R
nail prints

15. **Jesus**
R-in-L / L-in-R
nail prints

said,
R
tell, speak

"Not
R
don't

my
R-on-B
mine
[touch chest]

will
W + law

but
BHA / WA
however

thine
(possessive)

be

done."

16. Jesus
nail prints
R-in-L / L-in-R

delivers
D + save

from

temptation
WA
tempted
elbow

and
RHA / L→R

demons.
Satan + spirits

17. **The**

Lord
R
L + royalty

is

my
R-on-B
mine
[touch chest]

1. 2. 3.
scissors cut wool
R-on-L
Shepherd
1. sheep + 2. keep + 3. person

and
RHA / L→R

the

Lamb
sheep + small,

of

God.
R

18. **He**

leads
[L pulls R]

me

beside
near

the

still
quiet, calm

waters.
R / WF
W + flow

19.

Thy
(possessive)

RHA

rod
[*O* hands]

RHA / L→R

and

thy
(possessive)

R→F

staff,
holding staff

they

R-on-L

comfort
cupped hand

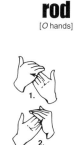

me.

20.

Thou

preparest
[*P* hands]

a

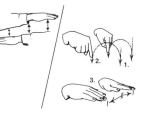

table
rest arm on table / 4 legs and a top

before
in front of, presence of,
presence

me,

and
RHA / L→R

mercy
pity, compassion
feel + sympathy

shall
will, would

follow
[R follows L]

me

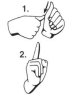

1.

2.

each

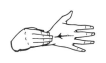
RHA / L→R

and

every
2X
[R *A* hand down L thumb]

RHA

day.

Practice Sentences

1. He was convicted about his sins Sunday.
2. He promised to bring the idols to the house.
3. Jesus came to be our Deliverer.
4. The shepherd carried a staff.
5. The little lamb followed the Mennonite lady.
6. The Lutherans omitted some doctrine.
7. Some people pray to Satan.
8. Protestants have communion at Christmas.
9. The Mennonite man stood beside the lamb.
10. The Presbyterian had a baptismal service.
11. The shepherd used a staff to control sheep.
12. The devil has many demons.
13. Mennonites pray and worship together.
14. Christmas was a time of mercy.
15. Angels worship God in heaven.
16. Demons worship the devil in hell.
17. We ought to obey God's commandments.
18. Jesus is the lamb of God.
19. People come to church on Christmas day.
20. Protestants omit worshiping idols.
21. Mennonites illustrate praying.
22. The holiness of God convicted evil angels.
23. The shepherd is a symbol of the Lord.
24. The angels were at the ascension of Jesus.

New Signs List

Word	Synonym	Memory Aid	Sentence	Word	Synonym	Memory Aid	Sentence
Acts	—	—	2	illustrate	—	I + show	13
angels	—	—	5	images	—	—	7
anointing	—	—	6	lamb	—	sheep + small, scissors cut wool	17
ascension	—	stand + ascend	2	leads	—	—	18
baptism	—	—	3	Lord	—	L + royalty	17
beside	near	—	18	Mennonite	—	prayer bonnet ties	11
Bible	—	Jesus book	7	parables	—	—	13
chapter	—	—	2	preparest	—	—	20
Christmas	—	—	10	Presbyterian	—	—	10
command-ments	—	C + law	8	recorded	applied	—	2
Communion	—	wine + bread	14	rod	—	—	19
convicted	guilty	heart jabbed	9	scriptural	verse	—	6
deliver	—	D + save	12	shepherd	—	sheep + keep + person	17
demons	—	Satan + spirits	16	spoke	say, tell	—	3
denomina-tional	denomination	—	12	staff	—	holding staff	19
devil	Satan	—	4	ten	—	—	8
done	—	—	15	thine	—	—	15
each	—	—	20	thou	—	—	20
Easter	—	—	10	thy	—	—	19
eleven	—	—	2	tithe	—	1/10	9
every	—	—	20	trespass	—	break + law	1
evil	—	E + bad	1	truth	honest, true	—	13
follow	—	—	20	verse	Scripture	—	2
God's	—	—	1	warns	—	—	7
He (God)	—	—	18	waters	—	W + flow	18
hell	—	devil + fire	4	will	—	W + law	15
holy	—	H + clean	3	wings	—	—	5
idols	—	—	7	worshiping	adore	—	7

Lesson 28

1. Accepting
approve, approval

R-in-L / L-in-R
Jesus
nail print

R
Christ
C + royalty

R-in-L / 2X
sometimes
once in a while,
occasionally

L→R
brings
carries

√
persecution.
[strikes finger]

2.

√
BHA
Saving
safe, salvation

√
WA / R
grace

is

√
unworthy
not + W + important

√
favor.

3.

√
RHA / R-in-L / WA
Glory,
[shake hand as it rises]

√
hallelujah,
clap + win

I

am

R-on-L
on

R-on-B
my
mine
[touch chest]

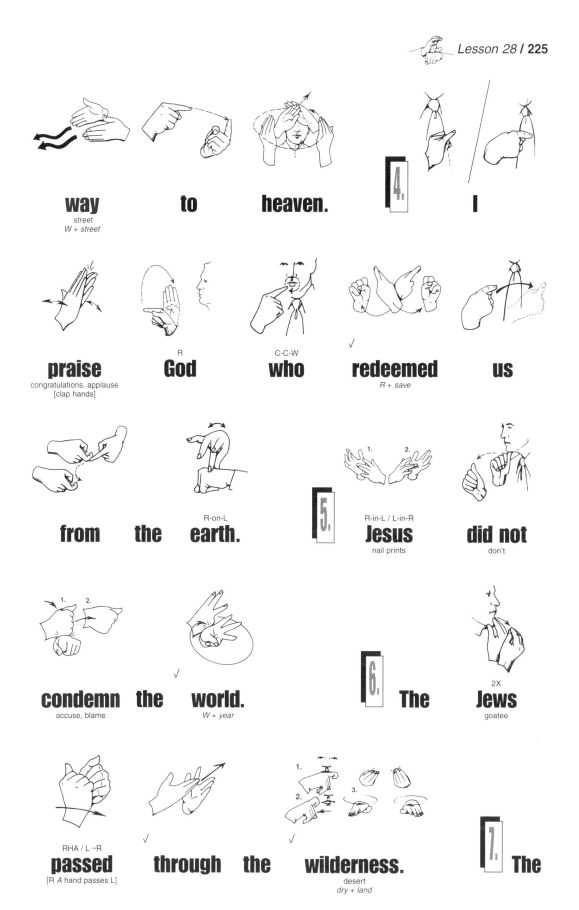

way
street
W + street

to

heaven.

4.

I

praise
congratulations, applause
[clap hands]

R
God

C-C-W
who

√
redeemed
R + save

us

from

the

R-on-L
earth.

5.

R-in-L / L-in-R
Jesus
nail prints

did not
don't

condemn
accuse, blame

√
the

world.
W + year

6.

The

2X
Jews
goatee

RHA / L→R
passed
[R A hand passes L]

√
through

the

√
wilderness.
desert
dry + land

7.

The

long

revival
thrill, excite,
enthrall
AA / IN

made
make
R-on-L

the

congregation
people + class
BHA / AA / IN

weary.
tired

8.

Jesus
nail prints
R-in-L / L-in-R

paid
RHA / R-in-L

the supreme
excellent
[*A* up]

price

for
WA

victory.
[*V* hands]

9.

It

will
shall, would

be a

thrilling,
enthrall, excited,
revival
IN / AA

wonderful
2X

time
wristwatch
R-on-L

in
R-in-L

heaven.

10.

We

can
could, able,
power

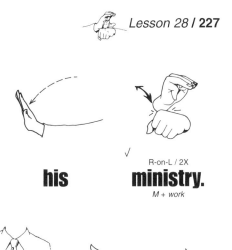

say
tell, speak

amen
R-in-L

to

his

ministry.
R-on-L / 2X
M + work

11. **We**

receive

this
now,
here

offering
R-in-L
earns + money

for
WA

world
W + year

missions.
R
missionary
[R *M* circled at L shoulder]

12. **Decisions**
judge, decide,
determine

  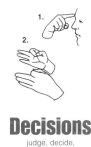

for
WA

Christ
R
C + royalty

are

for
WA

time
(age, historical)
[*T* hand]

  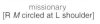

and
RHA / L→R

eternity.
CW
eternal, forever, infinity,
everlasting
always + still

13. **More**

people
BHA / IN / EA / AA
[*P* hands]

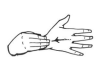  

need to | **be** | **sent** | **and** | **involved.**

EA / 2X
must, have to,
ought, should

√

RHA / L→R

√

R-in-L
including

---

14. **Jesus** | **was** | **born** | **among** | **the**

R-in-L / L-in-R
nail prints

√ WA / R-in-L / RHA / IN
birth

---

quiet | **hills** | **of** | **Bethlehem.**

still, calm

√

√ F→R
B + city

---

15. **The shepherds** | **saw** | **the** | **star** | **shining**

R-on-L
1. *sheep* + *keep* + 2. person

see

√ AA

√ WF

---

and | **were** | **fearful.** | **16.** **The**

RHA / L→R

afraid, frightened

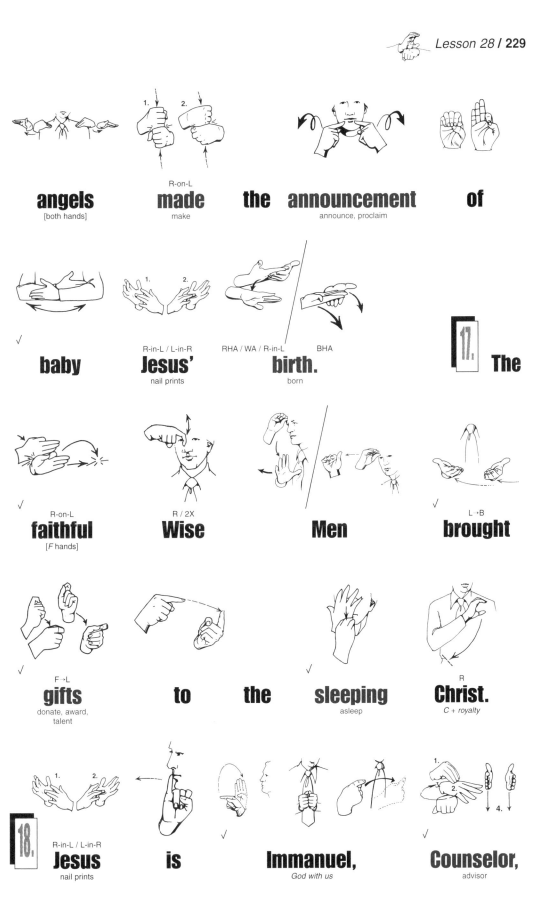

angels
[both hands]

R-on-L
made
make

the

announcement
announce, proclaim

of

√
baby

R-in-L / L-in-R
Jesus'
nail prints

RHA / WA / R-in-L   BHA
birth.
born

17.
The

√
R-on-L
faithful
[*F* hands]

R / 2X
Wise

Men

√
L→B
brought

√
F→L
gifts
donate, award,
talent

to

the

√
sleeping
asleep

R
Christ.
C + royalty

18.
R-in-L / L-in-R
Jesus
nail prints

is

√
Immanuel,
God with us

√
Counselor,
advisor

√ CW
the everlasting
forever, eternity, eternal,
infinity
always + still

√ BHA
Father.

19.

√
Jesus
nail prints

√ R-on-L
ministered
M + work

R-in-L
in

√
Judah,
Jews + land

BHA / WA
but
however

was

√ R-on-L
rejected.

20. **The**

√ R-in-L
risen
get up, resurrection

R
Christ
C + royalty

shall
will, would

√
descend
come down

with

power
might, strong

the

R / WA
second

R-on-L
time
(age, historical)
[*T* hand]

to

R-in-L / WA
begin
start, instituted,
initially

the

√
Millennium.
one thousand years

Practice Sentences

1. Jesus Christ has saving grace.
2. Praise the Lord, I am going to heaven.
3. The Jews passed through the wilderness.
4. Jesus was born in Bethlehem.
5. Angels announced the birth of Christ.
6. We gave our gifts to the baby yesterday.
7. His ministry is missions.
8. Bethlehem is a famous city.
9. The star is shining above.
10. They were sent into the wilderness.
11. We were weary in the wilderness.
12. He is faithful in his ministry.
13. The congregation is having revival.
14. Jesus gave us a thrilling victory.
15. They received many gifts in the offering.
16. Hallelujah for the grace that redeemed us.
17. The congregation paid their tithes.
18. The star was shining on Bethlehem.
19. The shepherd brought gifts.
20. We had a revival in Bethlehem.
21. The power of God's grace is thrilling.
22. Do not condemn those people.
23. The Wise Men brought gifts to Jesus.
24. The man shouted, "Amen!"

New Signs List

Word	Synonym	Memory Aid	Sentence	Word	Synonym	Memory Aid	Sentence
amen	—	—	10	need to	must, have to, ought, should, necessary	—	13
baby	—	—	16	offering	—	earns + money	11
Bethlehem	—	B + city	14	paid	—	—	8
born	birth	—	14	persecution	—	—	1
brought	—	—	17	redeemed	—	R + save	4
congregation	—	people + class	7	rejected	—	—	19
counselor	advisor	—	18	revival	thrill, excite, enthrall	—	19
descend	—	come down	20	risen	get up, resurrection	—	20
everlasting	forever, eternal, eternity, infinity	always + still	18	saving	safe, salvation	—	2
faithful	—	—	17	second	—	—	20
Father (God)	—	—	18	sent	—	—	13
favor	—	—	2	shining	—	—	15
gifts	donate, award, talent	—	17	sleeping	asleep	—	17
glory	—	—	3	star	—	—	15
grace	—	—	2	supreme	excellent	—	8
hallelujah	—	clap + win	3	thrilling	enthrall, excited, revival	—	9
hills	—	—	14	through	—	—	6
Immanuel	—	God with us	18	unworthy	—	not + W + important	2
Involved	Including	—	13	victory	—	—	8
Judah	—	Jews + land	19	weary	tired	—	7
Millennium	—	one thousand years	20	wilderness	desert	dry + land	6
ministered	—	M + work	19	wonderful	—	—	9
ministry	—	M + work	10	world	—	W + year	5,11

Lesson 29

 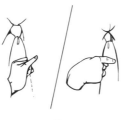 

1. ✓

Behold,　　　**I**　　　**stand**　　　**at**　　　**the**

R-on-L

[before]

 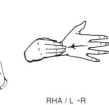  

door　　　**and**　　　**knock.**　　**2.** **Jesus**

RHA / L→R 　　R-on-L 　　R-in-L / L-in-R

✓　　✓　　nail prints

 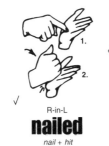

was　　**nailed**　　**to**　**the**　**cross**　**for**

R-in-L 　　　　　　　　WA

nail + hit

✓　　　　✓

1.

2.

our　　**sins.**　　**3.** **Jesus**　　**knew**

✓　　R-in-L / L-in-R 　　✓

known, knowledge,

aware, conscious

sorrow
sorry
[*A* over heart]
R-on-B

in
R-in-L

the

garden.
hoeing
→L / 2X

For
WA
4.

the knowledge
know, known,
aware, conscious

of

the

Lord
R
L + royalty

shall
will, would

fill
R-on-L

all
R-in-L

the

earth.
R-on-L

Rain
WF
5.

fills
R-on-L

the

rivers
WF
W + flow

that

flow
WF

into

the

ocean.
→R
sea
waves

We
6.

shall
will, would

praise
congratulations, applause
[clap hands]

and

adore
worship

our

dear
[*D* hands]

Lord.
R
L + royalty

7. **The**

beauty
C-C-W
pretty, lovely,
beautiful

of

the

soul
spirit, ghost

can
could, able,
power

be

seen

in
R-in-L

the

eyes.

8. **I**

sing
song

because

I

am

happy
2X
glad, rejoice

I

heard
listen
C at R ear

about
CW

✓

Pentecost.

9. **There** **is** **no**
none

sin

or

shame

in
R-in-L

heaven,

only
C-C-W / EA
alone, someone

✓

righteousness.
[R + clean]

10. **The** **Christian's**
Christ + person
Jesus + person

or

walk **is** **narrow**
BHA / AA
steps

but
BHA / WA
however

rich
money + pile

and
RHA / L→R

✓

precious.

11. **My**
R-on-B
mine
[touch chest]

journey
R / OUT
travel, trip

shall
will, would

end | **at** | **the** | **throne** | **in** | **the**
final, last | | | *chair* + arms | R-in-L |

Kingdom. | **This** | **generation** | **might**
king + *land*, soil | now, here | BHA / AA / R →L | AA / possibly, maybe, perhaps

12.

be | **alive** | **when** | **the** | **trumpet** | **calls.**
| life / WF / BHA | RHA | BHA | 2X / RHA | R-on-L

13. **The** | **sun** | **and** | **moon** | **rise**
| | RHA / L→R | |

over | **the** | **land.** | **14.** **Death** | **shall**
above / R-O-L | | *soil* + *plain* | dead, turnover / F→R | will, would

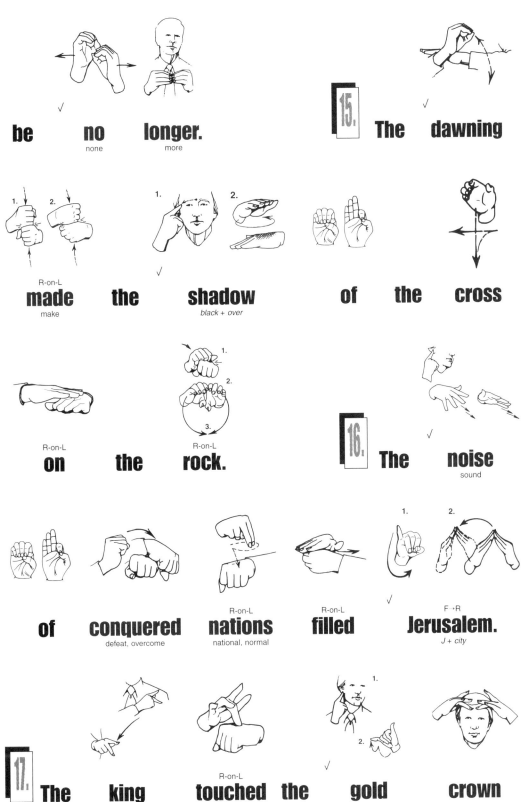

be **no** **longer.**
none / more

15. **The** **dawning**

made **the** **shadow** **of** **the** **cross**
R-on-L / black + over
make

on **the** **rock.** **16.** **The** **noise**
R-on-L / R-on-L / sound

of **conquered** **nations** **filled** **Jerusalem.**
defeat, overcome / national, normal / F→R
R-on-L / R-on-L / J + city

17. **The** **king** **touched** **the** **gold** **crown**
K - royalty / R-on-L / ear + yellow / [R & L thumb & center fingers grasp crown & put on head]

RHA / L→R
and

smiled.
cheery
[make a smile]

18.

He

did
do, doing

a

second

bow

RL
after
across

they

were

gone.

19.

The

chains
links

disappeared
vanished, solved problem

R-in-L
in

a

strange
odd

way.
street

20.

The

BHA
Pharisees,
[*P*s in square on chest]

really

R-on-L
hypocrites,

threw

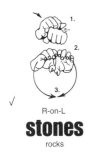
√
R-on-L
stones
rocks

√
R-on-L
upon

his

body.

Practice Sentences

1. I adore the beauty of the moon.
2. The journey to Jerusalem was long.
3. You can smile in your sorrow.
4. The trumpet shall sound when we conquer.
5. You should feel ashamed when you sin.
6. The river flowed into the ocean.
7. We praise and adore the Savior.
8. Behold the land of Jerusalem.
9. Do you know about the gold nail?
10. Jerusalem is a precious city.
11. People praised God on the day of Pentecost.
12. Behold the beauty of the sun and moon.
13. The rock made a shadow on the land.
14. Adore the beauty of Jerusalem.
15. The precious trumpet was gold.
16. At dawn they nailed the cross together.
17. America has many oceans, rocks, and rivers.
18. Grace is given to us from Christ.
19. Jesus' last journey led Him to Jerusalem.
20. Eternal life is a precious gift from God.
21. God is the Judge. Have you chosen Jesus?
22. Things happened after the death of Jesus.
23. Isaiah preached with a vision.
24. God is no myth to believers.

New Signs List

Word	Synonym	Memory Aid	Sentence	Word	Synonym	Memory Aid	Sentence
alive	life	—	12	Pentecost	—	—	8
behold	—	—	1	Pharisees	—	—	20
bow	—	—	18	precious	—	—	10
cross	—	—	2	rain	—	—	5
dawning	—	—	15	rich	—	money + pile	10
dear	—	—	6	righteousness	—	—	9
eyes	—	—	7	rise (sun)	—	—	13
fill	—	—	4,5	rivers	—	W + flow	5
flow	—	—	5	seen	—	—	7
gold	—	ear + yellow	17	shadow	—	black + over	15
gone	—	—	18	shame	—	—	9
hypocrites	—	—	20	sing	song	—	8
Jerusalem	—	J + city	16	sins	—	—	2,9
knew	knowledge, known, aware, conscious	—	3	smiled	cheery	—	17
knock	—	—	1	stones	rocks	—	20
land	—	soil + plain	13	strange	odd	—	19
moon	—	—	13	sun	—	—	13
nailed	—	nail + hit	2	threw	—	—	20
narrow	—	—	10	throne	—	chair + arms	11
noise	sound	—	16	trumpet	—	—	12
no longer	more	—	14	upon	—	—	20

Lesson 30

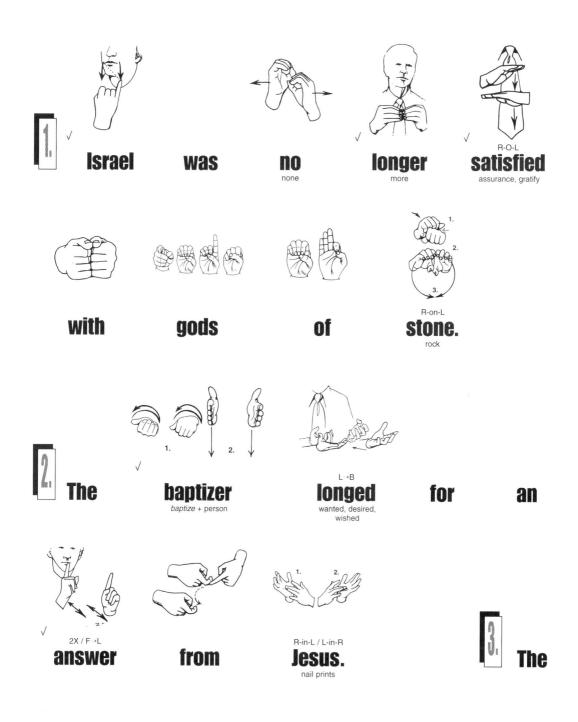

1. ✓

Israel

was

no
none

longer
more

satisfied
R-O-L
assurance, gratify

with

gods

of

stone.
R-on-L
rock

2. **The**

✓ **baptizer**
baptize + person

longed
L→B
wanted, desired,
wished

for

an

✓ **answer**
2X / F→L

from

Jesus.
R-in-L / L-in-R
nail prints

3. **The**

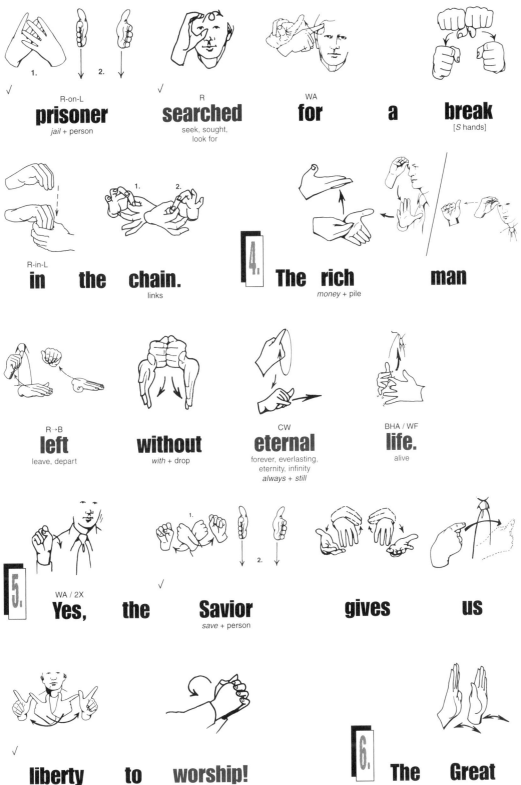

√ **prisoner**
R-on-L
jail + person

√ **searched**
R
seek, sought,
look for

for
WA

a

break
[*S* hands]

in
R-in-L

the

chain.
links

4. **The** **rich**
money + pile

man

left
R→B
leave, depart

without
with + drop

eternal
CW
forever, everlasting,
eternity, infinity
always + still

life.
BHA / WF
alive

5. **Yes,**
WA / 2X

the

√ **Savior**
save + person

gives

us

√ **liberty**
L + free

to

worship!
adore

6. **The** **Great**

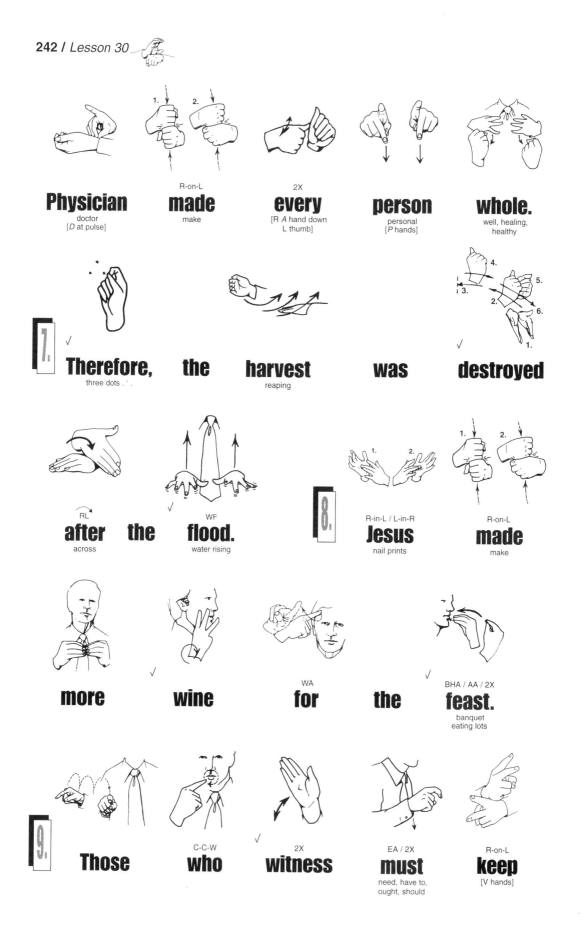

Physician
doctor
[*D* at pulse]

R-on-L
made
make

2X
every
[R *A* hand down
L thumb]

person
personal
[*P* hands]

whole.
well, healing,
healthy

7. √
Therefore,
three dots . ˙.

the

harvest
reaping

was

destroyed
√

after
across
RL

the

flood. √
WF
water rising

8.

R-in-L / L-in-R
Jesus
nail prints

R-on-L
made
make

more

wine √

for
WA

the √

feast.
BHA / AA / 2X
banquet
eating lots

9.
Those

C-C-W
who

√
2X
witness

EA / 2X
must
need, have to,
ought, should

R-on-L
keep
[V hands]

a **cheery**
smile
[5 hands]

R
attitude.
A at heart

10.

One

truly
verily

RHA / WA / R-in-L BHA
born
birth

R-in-L
again

will
shall, would

CW
always
ever

WA / R-in-L
pay

R
tithes.
1/10

11.

R-in-L / L-in-R
Jesus'
nail prints

BHA
mother,

Mary,

was

pregnant
[5 hands]

by

the

Holy

Spirit.
soul, ghost

12.

We

EA / 2X
should
need, have to,
ought, must

BHA / AA
walk
steps

after **the** **Spirit,** **not** **after** **the** **flesh.**
(follow)   soul, ghost   don't   (follow)

13. **We** **owe** **God** **much** **for**
√   debt, bill,   R   a lot of, amount   WA
afford   [comparative or quantity]

removing **our** **sin.** **14.** **There**
√   R-on-L   R
abortion

was **no** **place** **to** **bury** **Jesus.**
none   [P hands]   grave   R-in-L / L-in-R
mound of soil over grave   nail prints
√

15. **The** **young** **man** **was** **cross**
2X   √
youth   angry

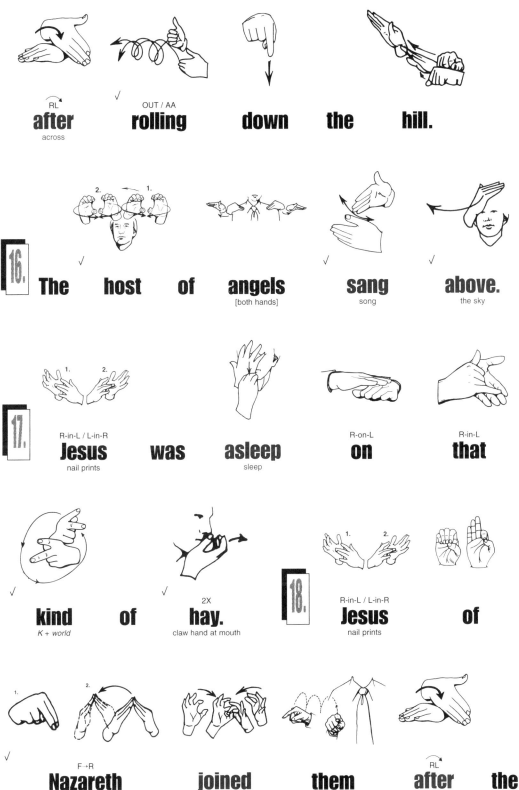

RL
after
across

√ OUT / AA
rolling

down

the

hill.

16. √
The

host

of

angels
[both hands]

√
sang
song

√
above.
the sky

17.
R-in-L / L-in-R
Jesus
nail prints

was

asleep
sleep

R-on-L
on

R-in-L
that

√
kind
K + world

of

√ 2X
hay.
claw hand at mouth

18.
R-in-L / L-in-R
Jesus
nail prints

of

√ F→R
Nazareth
N + city

joined
linked, hold

them

RL
after
across

the

Resurrection.
R-in-L
get up, risen

19.

Sinners

plunged
dive, dove

beneath **the** **flood** **lose** **all** **their**
R-U-L WF R-in-L
under water rising

guilty **stains.** **20.** **We** **are**
R / 2X R-in-L
convicting
heart jab

adopted **into** **the** **family** **of** **God**
assumed, BHA R
Rapture F + class

with **Him.**
(Jesus)

Practice Sentences

1. The sinner and the physician had wine.
2. The woman laid her gift on the stone altar.
3. The rich man searched for Jesus.
4. Jesus rose from the grave.
5. We are adopted into the family of God.
6. He accepted the cross as his symbol of love.
7. Everyone came to the feast.
8. The physician said she was pregnant.
9. The Savior searched for the lost sheep.
10. Only Jesus can satisfy your soul.
11. Israel is still searching for the Savior.
12. The guilty prisoner was put in jail.
13. Christians are forgiven because of the cross.
14. The congregation broke bread together.
15. We harvested the hay before the flood.
16. The angel spoke to the devil.
17. Always let God's will be first in your life.
18. We adopted the little boy who was asleep.
19. I joined the host of Israel for the harvest.
20. They jumped into the hay.
21. The prisoner's sins were removed.
22. The physician had a cheery attitude.
23. The woman destroyed the chair at the feast.
24. Her mother sang in the choir.

New Signs List

Word	Synonym	Memory Aid	Sentence	Word	Synonym	Memory Aid	Sentence
above	the sky	—	16	Nazareth	—	*N + city*	18
adopted	assumed, Rapture	—	20	owe	debt, bill, afford	—	13
after	—	—	12	place	—	—	14
answer	—	—	2	plunged	dive, dove	—	19
baptizer	—	*baptize + person*	2	pregnant	—	—	11
cross	angry	—	15	prisoner	—	*jail + person*	3
destroyed	—	—	7	removing	abortion	—	13
feast	banquet	eating lots	8	rolling	—	—	15
flood	—	water rising	7	sang	song	—	16
gods	—	—	1	satisfied	assurance, gratify	—	1
hay	—	claw hand at mouth	17	Savior	—	*save + person*	5
Him (Jesus)	—	—	20	searched	seek, sought, look for	—	3
host	—	—	16	sinners	—	—	19
Israel	—	—	1	stains	—	—	19
kind	—	*K + world*	17	therefore	—	three dots	7
liberty	—	*L + free*	5	wine	—	—	8
longer	more	—	1	witness	—	—	9

Word Index

*Word is listed as a synonym.

*Word is listed as a synonym.

*Word is listed as a synonym.

*Word is listed as a synonym.

	Lesson	Sentence		Lesson	Sentence		Lesson	Sentence
humble	15	20	in the past*	6	18	Korea	15	13
hundred	22	2	into	25	1	Korean	21	18
hungry	13	7	introduce	2	19			
hunt	20	7	invented	17	3	**L**		
hurried	18	8	involved	28	13	labor*	3	10
hurt	10	14	Ireland	6	15	ladder*	18	6
husband	6	12	iron (noun)	21	9	lady	8	13
hypocrites	29	20	iron (verb)	20	5	lamb	27	17
			is	1	11	land	29	13
I			Isaiah	26	19	language	3	2
I	1	3	island	23	3	large	7	7
ice cream	7	3	Israel	30	1	last (final)	9	18
ice skating	7	17	it	1	11	last (past)	8	20
idea	16	4	Italian*	6	15	last year	9	20
idiom	23	20	Italy	6	15	late	5	19
idle*	6	6				later*	9	17
idol	27	7	**J**			laugh	10	20
if	9	7	jail	23	1	law	8	1
ignorant	14	1	Jamaica	25	14	lazy	14	15
illustrate	27	13	Japan	15	13	leads	27	18
illustration	24	13	jealousy	17	8	learning	3	19
images	27	7	jelly	14	5	leave (abandon)	6	1
imagination	16	5	Jerusalem	29	16	leave (depart)	4	17
imagine* (verb)	16	5	Jesus	26	8	lecture*	26	13
Immanuel	28	18	Jewish	5	6	led	18	9
immediate*	5	8	job*	3	10	left* (abandon)	6	1
important	18	11	join*	23	6	left* (depart)	4	17
impress	18	14	journey*	6	14	left (direction)	12	15
improving	19	13	joy	26	7	lemon	11	2
in	3	13	Judah	28	19	lemonade	12	10
in a few days	16	15	judge (person)	17	17	lend	19	16
in charge of	26	11	judged	16	19	lesson	4	6
including*	28	13	jumping	18	3	let	9	7
India	23	19	just (exact)	9	4	let's	5	18
Indian	25	13	just* (right)	12	3	letter	4	4
individual	21	6				liar	14	20
infinity*	28	12	**K**			liberty	30	5
influence	17	2	Kansas City	9	12	lie down	18	3
inform*	16	8	keep	3	11	life	16	5
information	16	8	keys	12	20	light	11	4
in front of*	17	17	kill	25	6	lightbulb	22	1
initially*	6	7	kind (emotion)	10	17	lightning	20	19
innocent	17	17	kind (type)	30	17	like* (enjoy)	1	8
insist*	16	6	king	21	15	like (prefer)	3	2
instead	19	1	kingdom	26	12	like (same)	24	20
instead of*	24	6	kissed	17	5	limited	3	13
instituted*	6	7	kitchen	14	10	Lincoln	16	12
institution	22	20	kneel	18	4	line up	18	10
intelligent	15	1	knew	29	3	link*	23	6
intend*	10	19	knife	21	9	lion	25	4
interest	8	1	knock	29	1	lip-read	20	10
interpreter	19	4	know	5	6	list	22	18
interpreting	19	13	knowledge*	5	6	listen*	4	19
interrupt	13	19	known*	5	6	little	14	6

*Word is listed as a synonym.

*Word is listed as a synonym.

*Word is listed as a synonym.